The Chronicles of the Canons Regular of Mount St. Agnes

written by
Thomas À Kempis.

Translated by
J. P. Arthur.

Τι δητα οιομεθα, ει τω γενοιτο αυτο το καλον ιδειν, ειλικρινες καθαρον, αμικτον, αλλα μη αναπλεων σαρκων τε ανθρωπινων και χρωματων και αλλης πολλης φλυαριας θνητης, αλλ' αυτο το θειον καλον δυναιτο μονοειδες κατιδειν.

TRANSLATOR'S NOTE

The Chronicle of Mount St. Agnes is the only work of Thomas à Kempis of which no English translation has yet appeared, and even in its original form the book is not readily accessible to readers, since the only text is that published by Peter and John Beller of Antwerp in 1621. The ordinary collections of the works of à Kempis do not contain the Chronicle, although there is no doubt as to the authenticity of the book, which is of considerable importance to students of the movement known as "The New Devotion," and to those who are interested in the Brotherhood of the Common Life. The last nine pages of the Latin text have been added by an anonymous writer, and carry on the chronicle from the year 1471, in which à Kempis died, to 1477, but since this portion of the book is included in the first printed edition, and contains a notice of the author written by a contemporary member of the community, I have included the addition in the present translation of the Chronicle.

The Mother House of the Chapter to which the Monastery of Mount St. Agnes belonged, was the Monastery at Windesheim, of which we have a full account from the pen of John Buschius, a younger contemporary of à Kempis. This work is too long to be included in the present volume, although the Antwerp edition before mentioned puts the two Chronicles together; Busch's "Chronicon Windesemense" will therefore appear separately; but as the account of the foundation of the Mother House, written by William Voern, or Vorniken, supplements the information given by à Kempis, a translation of it is annexed to this book. The writer was Prior of Mount St. Agnes before his promotion to the same office in the Superior House, and it was under his rule that à Kempis spent the early years of his priesthood, those years in which he composed the first part at least of the great work with which his name is associated. William Vorniken also tells in outline the story of the conversion of the Low Countries to Christianity by Anglo-Saxon missionaries, and for all these reasons it has been thought that his "letter" may be of interest to English readers.

It will be seen that the spelling of proper names is both peculiar and variable, but the principle observed in this translation has been to adopt the spelling given in the text, except in cases where variation is evidently the result of a printer's error, and in those instances in which the writer *translated* names, *e.g.*, Hertzogenbosch appears in the Chronicle as Buscoducis, and Gerard is called sometimes Groote, Groot, or Groet, and sometimes Magnus.

Further accounts of the lives of some of the Brothers who are mentioned in this Chronicle may be found in a translation of another work of à Kempis published last year, and entitled "The founders of the New Devotion," Kegan Paul, Trench, Trübner & Co.; and the history of the other houses of the Chapter to which the Monastery of Mount St. Agnes belonged, has been treated exhaustively by Dr. J. G. R. Acquoy, "Het Klooster te Windesheim." Utrecht, 1880.

For the English reader the best accounts of the Brotherhood and of à Kempis himself, are the works of Rev. S. Kettlewell and Sir F. R. Cruise. The former, however, is quite unreliable as a translator, and draws untenable deductions from extracts whose purport he has misunderstood; but the latter is both accurate and interesting, being in fact the leading English authority on the subject which he has made his own.

PREFACE.

The pious desire of certain of our Brothers hath constrained me to put together a short chronicle concerning the beginning of our House, and the first foundation of our Monastery on Mount St. Agnes, that the said chronicle may be a comfort to them that are now alive, and a memorial for them that come after. Wherefore humbly assenting to their pious desires, I have gathered together a few things out of many, and these I have seen with mine own eyes, or have heard from the Elders of our House, or else have gathered from the writings of others.

Some of the Elders who first dwelt in this House have told us that or ever there was a monastery builded in this place, and before any man had yet come hither to serve God, there did often appear to the shepherds and to them that dwelt near, visions of men in white raiment who seemed to go in procession round the mount: and the signification and meaning hereby portended became clear enough afterward as time went by, when the monastery by God's grace begun in this place by a few Brothers and afterward finished with much toil came into being and a great company of Brothers dwelt therein—for then it was seen how the Devout Congregation of Canons Regular being clad in white raiment did serve God with devotion, singing hymns and psalms and celebrating Mass; also reciting the proper Canonical Hours to His praise every day, and praying for our benefactors, both living and dead, especially for them that are buried in this Monastery.

THE CHRONICLE OF THE CANONS REGULAR OF MOUNT ST. AGNES.

CHAPTER I

Of the first founders of the Monastery at Mount St. Agnes, and how Master Gerard Groote first pointed out this place to them

The House of Mount St. Agnes, which lieth outside the walls of the town of Zwolle, and on the eastern side thereof, had its origin and completion in this way.

The place used to be called in the vulgar tongue Mount Nemel and lieth not far from Zwolle, but one may traverse the distance in the space of an hour. Now there were in the State of Zwolle certain faithful men who had been turned wholly to God by Master Gerard Groote. These men had builded them an house, in a suburb belonging to the city, near an ancient Convent of Béguines, and here they served God humbly and with devotion. Amongst these the chief was John of Ummen, a man dedicated to God, and greatly beloved by Gerard; and with him there abode likewise Wychmann Rurinch, Reyner, son of Leo of Renen, and two or three others that were well disposed. Moreover, a certain Clerk that dwelt in those parts named Wittecoep, had joined himself to them and lived among them devoutly. There was also the mother of John of Ummen, named Regeland, a widow of ripe age, who ministered to the necessities of these servants of God, giving good heed to the care of the house as a faithful Martha. Most gladly would she listen to the Word of God, and, like Mary, was never sated with the sweetness of the Holy Scriptures that were read.

When any one at meal-time read somewhat incorrectly and stammered over the words, this venerable woman said to him "Read no more and do not defile the Word of God lest harm come to holy things and they that hear be offended in thee. Let another read that hath better skill thereto, that we may all understand and be edified."

After no long time this good woman came to the end of her life on the Thursday in Holy Week after Mass was ended, and she was buried at Zwolle by her friends and the Brothers. From that hour and day, for three whole days, her son John Ummen fasted from every kind of food to promote his mother's salvation, and he neither ate nor drank aught until the dawning of the day of the Lord's Passover, and yet was he as whole in body and in strength as if he had been well fed every day.

And as these servants of God lived in poverty and at the common charge it came to pass that many men that were in the world, considering their holy life, came together to them, being eager to serve God and to leave the world, in the hope of an eternal gain. Meanwhile it happened that the venerable Master Gerard Groote came to Zwolle about the beginning of Lent, and of necessity abode there certain days, since he was anxious to comfort his poor children, for it was his desire to refresh with the word of consolation those whom he had drawn to leave the world. So a very great company of people came together to his preaching, and many devoutly submitted themselves to his counsel, for sometimes he would preach two sermons in one day so as to water the chosen vineyard of the Lord. And if he had determined to preach after the midday meal, he would remain praying in the Church or walking in meditation in the churchyard, taking no food himself, while he awaited the return of the people. For this reason they that loved his holy discourse were unwilling to stay away too long, but would sit them down in the churchyard or in the Church, and take beforehand places that were convenient and near the pulpit, so that at the proper hour they might the more readily hear and understand the Word of God. And when Gerard had done his faithful preaching, each would return to his own concerns rejoicing with eager heart, and praising God for all the things he had heard. And they marvelled above measure at the humble bearing of the Master, and were edified thereby, that he, a man of so great fame and knowledge, one that had friends great and famous, should go about the streets with so meek an aspect, and showing little care for his attire; for he cared not at all about worldly things, and sought only to gain a great usury of souls for God. He was well favoured, kindly in word, and courteous to all, so that any man whatever, whether a stranger or born in the land, even though poor and unknown, might speak to him and receive from him some discourse upon the things of God. The good saw this and rejoiced thereat, but the froward gnashed with their teeth and spake evil of Gerard. A certain man, therefore, one of the great ones of the State, came near to him, and rebuked his words and deeds, for the man himself took more pleasure at that time in worldliness than in the things of God. "Why," said he, "dost thou disquiet us, and bring in new customs? Cease from this preaching, and do not disturb or frighten men." But Gerard made answer with wisdom and constancy: "I would not willingly suffer you to go to Hell," and the man said again with indignation: "Let us go thither in peace," but the kindly and good Master replied: "I will not do so; if thou wilt not hear, there will be some who will gladly give ear"—but we must return to our history.

When the most beloved Master was sojourning in Zwolle for the purpose of preaching the Word, some of his disciples aforementioned who dwelt together there came to him secretly and confessed that they desired to live a life further removed from that of the world, for they could not bear to mingle with worldlings without suffering hurt to their spiritual life; and they said that they would choose to dwell without the City if he should agree thereto. They begged him therefore, as loving sons speaking to their father, to condescend to go with them some little space outside the City to look for a place convenient wherein to live quietly. Then Gerard assented to their pious prayers, and when the next day dawned he prepared for the journey and taking with him the brothers Wychmann, Reyner, Henry and James Wittecoep, he went with them towards the mountains of Nemel to a place that was foreordained of God, and separated from the multitude; for men were seldom seen to come thither or to pass by, and patches of thorns and nettles grew here and there upon the hills and valleys. So as they went forth the wind beat against them, but neither rain nor wind could stay the Master from the straight course, and he went on rejoicing and said pleasantly to his companions: "I will go before you and shield you from the wind with my cloak." But as they drew near to the place, they went up to the top of an hill, and having made a circuit round the mountains for some little space, they at last beheld a valley, that was narrow and deep, upon the northern side of the mountain, and Gerard's disciples asked him a question, saying: "See! most beloved Master, how good is this place, and how private; here we may hide for the love of Christ, as of old the holy Eremites did hide in the mountains and in caves in the earth." But this they said in simplicity of heart out of the fervent zeal of their devotion, and their desire for a life more remote from the world, for they thought there they could be hid, screened by the thickets of brushwood. But the Master being most discreet and wise in counsel soon dissuaded them from this purpose, for a place that lieth low doth never suit the human complexion, nor would a place so narrow avail in future for many men to dwell in. So they withdrew their feet prudently therefrom and visited another mountain that was near; and their wise leader saw that on the south side thereof was a level place fit for crops, and he said to them that stood by: "Place your tabernacle at the foot of this mountain—then shall ye be able to make a little garden for your herbs and fruits on the level place toward the south. If the Lord grant me life I will be here often with you." Having visited this place and walked about it through God's inspiration, they returned again to the City together, leaving the issue of the matter to the pleasure of the Almighty. But in the same year the beloved Master Gerard, that light and lamp of devotion that shone upon his country of Utrecht, was taken away from this world to receive the reward of his labours, and he went up from the vale of our lamentations to the mount of everlasting bliss.

CHAPTER II.

Of the building of the first House on Mount St. Agnes.

But after the passing of the Master, who must ever be held in remembrance, the new branch of his planting ceased not to bear fruit; moreover the heaven shed dew upon it from above, as Gerard at the end of his life had promised, so that our land yielded increase in her season; and the men above named continued to carry into effect the intention which they had formed in their minds. The chief mover in this holy work was James Wittecoep, the son of one Thomas Coep, a man who had been a magistrat in the town of Zwolle; and he did all that in him lay to promote the foundation of an house on the mountain for the servants of God. Goswin Tyasen, who afterward became a Canon Regular at Windesheim, assisted him in this business, for he, relying upon the goodness of God, and having the ear of his fellows, was eagerly desirous to move them to choose this place. There were others also of like purpose, but these two were the chief men amongst them, and they all relied upon the help of their friends, but especially upon the co-operation of the mercy of God by Whose nod all things are determined. Therefore they besought the heritors of Bercem and Nemel, joint owners of the farm, to grant them a portion of the land, and the site where now the Monastery is builded, and the owners thereof did freely grant their request and gave them the land for the Brothers to dwell in. When they had obtained the power to build upon the spot pointed out to them aforetime by Master Gerard, they set in order a small house, at the bottom of the mountain, that had been given to them by a certain matron, and some labourers assisted them in this work. This house was builded of logs and earth, but was only roofed in above with common thatch. But when this poor little habitation, on an humble site on the lower part of the mountain was builded, no man dwelt there, because it lacked household stuff; yet certain of the Brothers whose hearts were set on the completion of the work would visit it, and sometimes one or two would sleep upon the straw there, in their clothes, but for their food they either brought somewhat with them or returned to their friends in the town.

Scarce have I known of any place or house that was begun in so great poverty, and yet came, in despite of divers hindrances, to so great an increase of prosperity; but Jesus our Saviour Himself began in the deepest poverty, and His lack did make rich Holy Church. This house therefore, poor at first, unknown and hidden, did deserve in process of time to be more widely increased through the blessing of our Father in Heaven, Who doth ever turn His Face toward lowly things, but doth look from afar upon the lofty. For as wealthier persons came and brought their goods into the common stock, the place whose beginning was so poor, and its outward appearance so lowly, grew to be a yet fairer vineyard of the Lord of Sabaoth. For the tillers of the farm and the country folk of the land of Bercem and Nemel, seeing that an house was now built on the mountain and that devout men had come together there to serve God in humility and simplicity, gave and assigned to them and their successors the aforesaid place in honour of Holy Religion, and that prayers might be offered for them and their friends; which grant they did also confirm in writing to any others whom God Almighty should see fit to associate with them. In regard to this holy gift and this pious request made by consent of the owners of the place, there was but one deed executed relating to the first and original foundation. This is attested by the seals of many honest men, and in it is given a short description of the manner of the Common Life and of the wholesome rule so far as this same was applicable to the conditions of the Brotherhood in the early days. These things were done and finished in the year of the Lord 1386 on the Friday before Palm Sunday, and a year and a half after the death of the aforesaid Master Gerard.

CHAPTER III.

Concerning the names of the first Brothers and their labours.

These are the names of those first Brothers, the devout men who began to build the House of Mount St. Agnes and to dwell there. First James Wittecoep, the chief promoter of our House and the earnest keeper thereof in all things. He afterward became a Priest in Zwolle and served the Altar in the Hospice there, where he died after making a good confession. Secondly, there was John Ummen, son of Assetrin, whose mother was called Regeland. He, though blind and unlettered, was yet the familiar friend and devout disciple of Master Gerard, and he became the first Rector of the House, being a good man and a comfortable. Thirdly, there was Wychmann Roerinck van Hellender, a pattern of poverty and patience; he, putting aside his friends, who were many, became an humble hearer of Gerard, and was Procurator to this poor little congregation.

Other upright men also were joined to these chief Brothers, being drawn to give up the world by the sweet savour of the reputation of this new and holy congregation. Their names are worthy of the fame of a good memorial, for they were shining lights of holy poverty, obedience, continence, and daily toil. The first was Reyner, son of Leo of Renen of the diocese of Utrecht, who often made pilgrimages out of his devotion; but afterward became converted by Gerard's preaching and gave up the world. The second was Reyner the younger, a man without reproach, poor and accustomed to toil. He, too, came from Renen which is in the diocese of Münster. The third was called Gerard the cook, for he at the first was cook to the House, but afterward became the porter, a man fervent in deed, and devout in prayer, who was born at Deventer. All these knew Gerard Groote in the flesh, and often heard him preach the Word of God among the people. By these humble, simple-hearted, and devout little servants of Christ—these who did verily despise the world—was our House on mount Nemel begun, which House after that it became a

Monastery was called Mount St. Agnes. Moreover by little and little several devout clerks and lay folk from the neighbouring towns and from far off districts came to join these men, and they earned their daily bread by the labour of their hands. For none was allowed to avoid his task, none might go about idly, neither did any dare to talk of worldly matters, but all were taught to labour for the common good, and to call often upon God in prayer at the appointed hours after the manner of the holy Fathers in Egypt: for these, too, did labour with their hands, but during the hours of toil they never ceased from prayer. Likewise they had received this rule from Master Gerard, that none ought to be accepted save such as were willing to labour with their hands and take part in the Common Life. Wherefore the clerks were diligent in writing the books of Holy Scriptures, and the lay folk busied them with bodily labour and tillage. Some also followed the tailor's craft, others wove wool and flax; others again made baskets and mats, or did divers tasks for the good of the community at the bidding of their Superior. Outwardly indeed they led a life of poverty and toil for Christ's sake, but the love of the heavenly life made sweet the present indigence. If one went forth on any business, he would first utter some short word concerning the things of God, or would speak the Name of Jesus, and some other would reply with "Christ" or "Mary" as his devotion impelled him. For a great while they lived together in this companionship, and until the time of the foundation of the Monastery, all alike, both Clerks and Lay folk obeyed their first Rector, John of Ummen, a zealous man and well skilled in spiritual things. With such diligence did they follow the virtue of obedience that none dared even to drive in a nail, or do any little thing without the knowledge of the Rector or Procurator, for they received fraternal correction by way of warning for the least neglect, nor was there given any place for excuse, but every man did humbly acknowledge his fault, and was forward to promise amendment. But if any were not ready to obey, or should cling stubbornly to what was good in his own eyes Father John would chide him more sternly as the manner of the fault and the quality of the person did demand. Sometimes fired with yet greater zeal for discipline and in order to affright the other Brothers he would say to some that were ill content, or slow to take his Orders: "Lo! the door standeth open. If any will go forth, let him go: I would rather have one that is obedient than many that are disobedient. By the favour of God I may readily find others who will cheerfully do what ye refuse." Thus by the voice of his authority he would curb the ill-contentment of some. Also he used to say that unwilling and sluggish Brothers were false prophets who thought that naught was profitable save what was good in their own eyes.

Once it happened that the elder Reyner was sent out with some other Brothers to guard the reeds, lest the cattle that passed by might chew and injure them. But when the time for the midday meal came all the rest went in, and Reyner alone remained on watch in the fields, and afterwards he, too, went in to take his sustenance. Then he was asked wherefore he had not come in with the others at the appointed hour, and he answered that he had remained outside thinking to do the more good thereby, and prevent danger to their stuff. But Father John replied, "Would that the beasts had despoiled all our goods so that thou hadst come in with the rest as in duty bound. This would have pleased me better." Then was Reyner deeply penitent, and groaning he prostrated himself humbly on the ground asking for pardon, and saying that he would never do the like again. But yet John was full of comfort and kindness to those that were tempted or oppressed with any weighty matter, for he had the gracious power of consoling all, whatever might be the cause for which they came to him. Master Gerard himself often sent divers persons to be instructed by him in the way of God, saying to them, "Go to blind John of Ummen, that devout and upright man, and whatsoever he saith unto you, do it." He also bore this witness about John, saying "That blind man hath better sight than all that are in Zwolle," meaning that though he lacked natural sight, yet was he illumined inwardly by the radiance of truth, and showed the way of eternal salvation to many that resorted to him, and gave them the guidance of the true light.

Among these early Brothers so great was the zeal of their love that each strove to surpass the other in doing work that was humble; and they were eager in lowly service one to the other. So while one was asleep another would rise up earlier than was customary and finish his work; but if any were somewhat slower in going forth to his labour, some other that was quicker would take his place, and it was often found that some task was finished though none knew who had done it. By this means was charity shown in deed, and humility of heart was preserved, according to the saying, "Love to be unknown."

All that dwelt in the House were stirred up by a like devotion to do menial tasks and fulfil humble offices. Wherefore the clerks and weavers would not avoid the work in the fields, but when called thereto at harvest time they would go forth with the rest to gather in the sheaves of corn. Following the rule of obedience, and acting for the common good, they made the hay, or dug the ground, or planted herbs, whenever such work must needs be done. So, too, holy David doth praise them that fear God, and doth minister sweet words of consolation to them that labour well, saying: "Thou shalt eat the labour of thy hands, well is thee and happy shalt thou be."

CHAPTER IV.

Of the scanty food and raiment of the Brothers, and how wondrously God did provide for them.

Who can tell how poor was their food while they laboured at their daily toil? Their victual was coarse, their drink ungenerous, their raiment simple and rude, so that naught did minister to the lusts of the flesh, but the needs of the body were satisfied soberly enough. They were often compelled to eat food that was of evil savour through lack of better victual; but constant toil and hunger made herbs and pulse to be pleasant to the taste. Fish was given to the community seldom, and eggs more rarely still, but yet of their goodwill the Brothers would give these to the sick, or to strangers, if by any means they could get such things. Wherefore one hath said, "When the reign of poverty is long, pleasure doth endure but a little space."

On certain days the rule allowed them to eat flesh meats, but if at such times a larger mess was set before them, yet was it not more daintily cooked. Furthermore, certain amongst them, who while they dwelt in the world had been taught to love a very different fare, were now content with scanty and coarse food, doing great violence to their lusts thereby; but yet they bore all these things patiently after that saying of Christ, "The Kingdom of Heaven suffereth violence, and the violent take it by force." Sometimes when supper was ended scarce aught did remain to be divided amongst them on the day following; at other times there was lack of utensils or cooking pots, or suitable food would fail; but God the Maker of all things, who of old did feed the people in the wilderness, did not desert the Brothers on the Mount. So it once came about that when they had consumed almost all their food, Gerard the cook being anxious for the morrow, made his lack known to Father John, saying sadly "What shall I set before them to-morrow?" But John consoled his sadness with kindly words, and exhorted him to have faith in the Lord, who doth not fail them that hope in Him. And when that day had drawn on to evening, Everard of Eza, Curate of Almelo, came unexpectedly in his chariot as if sent by God to comfort the poor. He was received by the Brothers eagerly and reverently, and they brought him in as if the Hospice was his own, for he loved the House and all that dwelt therein by reason of their utter poverty and their simple manner of life, and because their desire was to hinder none, but to profit all men; moreover he was united to Father John by a special bond of love. Wherefore, when he had determined to travel to Windesem, or had business at Zwolle, he delighted to come first to the Brothers on the Mount; and being a mighty shepherd of souls as well as a most skilful physician, he alighted from his carriage and fed souls that were in want thereof with the fodder of the Holy Word, and likewise cheered the faint of heart by giving them the food they lacked. He had brought with him fine meal, and flesh, and he gave the same to the Brothers for their common use; and they receiving the gifts he offered were all comforted by their better fortune, and gave thanks to God and to Everard that of his bounty he had provided for them and succoured them in their so great need. At another time, also, divers poor Clerks had been called from Zwolle to help them in some work, wherefore certain of the Brothers went down to fish in the brook Vecht, whose course is near to the mountain. So they let down their nets in the name of Jesus, and by the grace of God, who made all waters, there were taken of the fish called bream a number equal to the number of their guests.

At that time Gerard Bronchorst, a Canon of Utrecht, and a great friend to the devout, was in authority at Deventer, and he gave two cows to our Brothers on the Mount, but forasmuch as God would prove their patience and increase their faith, one of the cows died, though the other one remained whole. And the wondrous goodness of God provided that the one should give so large a yield of milk as to suffice for all the Brothers, though they would have thought that they would scarce get enough from two. Then was seen the fulfilment of the word of the prophet Esaias, who saith: "It shall come to pass in that day that a man shall nourish a young cow, and for the abundance of the milk he shall eat butter."

At the beginning of their common life the Brothers were despised by worldlings, and they bore patiently the derision of them that passed by; also they were called by vile names in scorn, and suffered much evil speaking and many injuries from the envious; but the patience of the good overcame the malice of the froward, and the freedom of their good conscience gave them the greater joy because of the scorn that was cast upon them. For although men that were ill-disposed would insult these poor little ones of Christ, and blushed not to speak evil of the innocent, yet many that feared God would praise their holy conversation; such men assisted them with kindly deeds and help, being moved thereto by pious reasons.

One of the community, a Lay Donate and an upright man, was employed in feeding the cattle, and as he was driving an herd of swine in the field he met an ancient crone, who began to abuse him and to hurl unseemly words at him. And the devout Brother answered her gently, saying, "Good dame, tell me my faults freely, and chide me sternly, for I greatly lack such chastisement," but the woman hearing this was smitten with inward remorse, and said in a changed voice: "What should it profit me to help you to the kingdom of heaven, but myself to hell!" for she perceived that by her chiding the Brother earned fresh merit, but she punishment for her frowardness.

It came to pass that as two of the Brothers were at work together out of doors, one by mischance did unwittingly hurt the other somewhat, and he who had done the injury prayed the other to pardon him for God's sake. But the Brother who was hurt in body was whole in heart, and said: "Even if thou hadst slain my father I would freely pardon thee," and those that stood by and heard his saying were edified, and glorified God for the gracious words that proceeded from the sufferer's mouth. May these few things that I have told of the early deeds of our elders be pleasing to the reader.

CHAPTER V.

Of the consecration of the first chapel and altar at Mount St. Agnes.

On the Vigil of the Feast of St. John the Baptist, and in the year of our Lord 1395, was consecrated the first chapel on the Mount of St. Agnes the Virgin, and the first altar therein was dedicated in honour of that saint, and of the most blessed Mary Magdalene, by Hubert, the Suffragan and Vicar-General for Pontifical Acts to our most Reverend Father and Lord, Frederic, Bishop of Utrecht.

And after the rite of Consecration, when the Dedication Festival was at hand, being the Sunday after the Nativity of St. John, Reyner, the Curate of Zwolle, came and was the first to sing a Solemn Mass in the chapel, wherein he offered the sacrifice of perpetual praise to God, for he was friendly disposed to the Brothers, and at unity with them. So from that day forward the Holy Mysteries of our Redemption were celebrated there by Priests and Clerks, and on festivals, hymns to the praise of God were sung to stir up devotion of heart.

Having made this holy beginning, the lowly band of Brothers was kindled to a still greater love of the worship of God, but in after time, when the new and larger church in the monastery was builded and consecrated, the dedication of this former chapel was transferred to the latter by licence of the Bishop, but as was more seemly, it was dedicated first to St. Mary and afterward to St. Agnes. After this, when nearly three years had gone by, the desire of the Brothers to build a monastery burned fiercely within them, and the elder amongst them especially, with their Rector, were eager to do this work and carry it forward with all speed, for certain urgent reasons did compel them. They saw that without monastic discipline the way of life in the House could not continue to be ordered duly, and therefore they determined that the habit of an holy order must be their refuge, for they were instant to make prudent provision for themselves and those that should come after, and to stop the mouths of them that spoke evil, because such men did strive with the cunning of this world to disturb the lowly and simple lives of the Brothers. Moreover, though they were still poor and had not things suitable to their need—either proper buildings or service books—yet did they try to begin the work, trusting in the mercy of God and heartened by the help of good men. And one spake of them and marvelled that men so poor should wish to build a monastery and to take religious vows, though they had no hope of increase, but Father John of Ummen, ever a lover of poverty, answered him, saying: "I have always heard from holy men that poverty is good, being both the cause of all good and the means of increasing the same."

CHAPTER VI.

Of the year and place in which the first four Brothers were invested.

In the year of the Lord 1398, on the 18th day of January, being the Feast of St. Prisca, Virgin and Martyr, our Right Reverend Lord Frederic of Blanckenhem, the renowned Bishop of Utrecht, issued his license to the devout priests, Egbert van Lingen, and Wolfard, the son of Matthias, and to the other Clerks and Lay Brothers that dwelt on Mount St. Agnes, in Nemel, near Zwolle, for it was his desire to increase the glory of God, and to promote the cause of Holy Religion. By the full authority vested in him he gave them leave to build a monastery for the Order of Canons Regular in any fit and proper place in his diocese, so that they might worthily and devoutly serve as the soldiers of Almighty God in the Regular Order, following the rule of the blessed Augustine. So having obtained this licence in their favour, they chose a place in the freehold land that is called Westerhof, in the district of Gherner and the parish of Dalvessen, the curate of which parish, who was an honourable man named Frederic Denter, giving his assent to their purpose. They determined to set their monastery here because they had found no other site that was fitting, although they sought anxiously elsewhere a place of habitation. At this time the men of Zwolle would not suffer a monastery to be built upon the Mount at Nemel, though this was done in after days by the favour of God, but Egbert Mulart had given them this land at Westerhof. He was a most upright man, and one in authority, being of gentle lineage in Hasselt, and he was a trusty friend and a special patron of the devout. Here then they built for their first need a small chapel, which they let consecrate in honour of Mary, the most Blessed Mother of God, and also other buildings of moderate size, and they reverently called the place "The Garden of the Blessed Mary," in honour of Christ's gentle Mother. When these things were done, the day drew nigh on which the Brothers of this

House should be invested there. Now on the day of the Lord's Annunciation, which is the solemn Feast of the Blessed Mary ever Virgin, Mother Church doth celebrate throughout all the world the first act of our Redemption. So that when that holy day had dawned with fair sunshine there came the Reverend Lord Hubert, Bishop of Yppuse, and Suffragan to our Lord Bishop of Utrecht, for he had been summoned thither upon that day. And when the waxen tapers and crosses and the other ornaments were ready, he there consecrated the burial ground, and the three altars, and then at the High Altar, which he had dedicated, he sung Mass with solemn music.

Afterward, in his reverend presence, and in the face of a large company of other religious, both Clerks and Lay, Brothers who had come together from every quarter to keep this Festival, the first four Brothers of our House were invested by that reverend and devout man, John Wale, Prior of the Regulars in the state of Zwolle, for he had been summoned for this very purpose. This number four did mystically signify the number of the four Evangelists, and the names of these Brothers, which are worthy to be cherished by them that come after, are here set down. The first was Brother Egbert of Lingen, who had been chosen for the priesthood by the Brothers on the Mount three years before this time.

The second was Brother Wolfard, son of Matthias of Medenblike, a priest of great age.

The third was John Ummen, a Clerk who came from Campen, a kinsman of John of Ummen, our first founder. The fourth was Dirk of Kleef, a Clerk who came from that state. These four made their profession on the same day, and when the Divine Mysteries had been celebrated, and their bodies had been refreshed, they spent the day in spiritual rejoicing and brotherly love. Brother Egbert was the Senior in standing and took the place of Rector of the House until a new Rector appointed by the Chapter should come; then he gave place to Brother Wolfard and stood humbly behind him. The Clerks who were not yet invested with the habit of the Order were these:—Wichbold, son of John of Deventer, Henry Huetinc of Deventer, John of Kempen, of the diocese of Cologne, Hermann of Kempen, of the same diocese.

After Easter, when a general Chapter was held by the Fathers at Windesem, these were received into the Order, and their names were set down and written as members of the Fellowship of Houses belonging to us: the Fathers also provided them a suitable Rector, and after a little space that religious and devout Brother, Egbert Lingen, was sent to them. He had been a member of the Monastery of St. Saviour, at Emsten, and for about a year, that is, until the coming of the new Prior, he ruled over the House, as will be shown hereafter. Throughout the summer of this same year the Pestilence was heavy at Deventer, Zwolle, Campen, and the neighbouring towns and districts, so that it often happened that twenty or thirty men were buried in one day in the divers parishes of these towns.

About this time and on the Feast of the Nativity of St. John the Baptist, died Reyner, Curate of Zwolle, and two priests that were his chaplains. He was a good man and pitiful to the poor, and ever cherished a special devotion to St. John the Baptist. At this time also died many devout persons, both men and women.

CHAPTER VII.

How the monastery was removed from Westerhof to Mount St. Agnes.

In the same year of the Lord 1398, on the 26th day of the month of August, two days before the Festival of our Holy Father Augustine, did that most kindly Lord Frederic, by the grace of God, Bishop of Utrecht, issue a further licence. He did ever most faithfully promote the interests of our House, and was our special patron, and he had compassion upon the Brothers who were invested a short time before at Westerhof, in that they were ill-content with the place, and ill-provided for there, by reason of divers hindrances and impediments that were not agreeable to the religious life. The Bishop therefore, hearing of these hindrances and the true causes thereof, gave them licence to transfer themselves and all their goods from the aforesaid place to Mount St. Agnes, so soon as might be convenient, and to retain the same rights and privileges as he had before conferred upon them. Thus for the second time they obtained his full and gracious consent to their desires, and Conrad Hengel, then Vice-Curate of Zwolle, likewise assented to their pious wishes.

Therefore on the eve of the day of the Exaltation of the Holy Cross they returned to the place that they had long possessed and where the greater number of their friends still continued to dwell, with blind John of Ummen; they left, however, some few Lay Brothers at Westerhof to arrange their affairs.

Moreover the Bishop of Utrecht had given them a licence for the consecration of a burial-ground for the use of the monastery that they should found on Mount St. Agnes. But when Hubert, the Bishop Suffragan, came for this purpose and entered into Zwolle, he was not allowed to continue his journey to the Mount until the Magistrates had first spoken with the Lord Bishop of Utrecht, for they thought to dissuade him from his opinion. From this cause the consecration of the burial-ground was delayed for the space of a year, until the return of the Bishop of Utrecht, for the said Bishop during the year had gone to the Curia at Rome, and he ordered that the cause of both parties should be put off and await his coming and presence on his return. But when he had come back from Rome and entered his own country in safety, certain of our Brothers came to him and asked him once more to give permission for the consecration of the burial-ground, and he, yielding to the importunity of his friends, did freely grant their petition. So he issued his commands again and ordered the consecration of this place, for he loved it and paid no heed to the complaints of the adversaries, since he preferred the honour of God and the progress of religion rather than the unjust words of worldlings, who, as is well-known, do often oppose the desires of good folk. From that time forward he showed special love to the House on the Mount, and extended to it yet fuller patronage, so that one day when he was riding round the mountain on his way to Zwolle, he asked one of his companions, saying: "What is this place, and what manner of men dwell here?" and his Vicar answered him: "Beloved Lord, dost thou not yet know that place? This is thy monastery, this is Mount St. Agnes, and the Brothers of the Mount dwell there." And the Bishop made answer: "It is well—may God preserve them."

It came to pass in this same year, 1398, in the month of September, when the Plague was still amongst us that a well-disposed Lay Brother named John, son of Faber, who was smitten with the pestilence, came from Zwolle to the mountain, and sought hospitality in the name of God. And being received in charity, his disease grew heavy upon him, and he died on the Feast Day of St. Maurice the Martyr. But after his death certain of the Clerks and Lay folk, being infected with the Plague, were taken from this life after a little while, but several others grew whole of their sickness, for the Lord had mercy upon them.

Lastly, on the day after the Feast of St. Francis the Confessor died John, son of Nicolas of Campen, a Lay Brother of great age, who had been the gardener.

On the day of the translation of our holy Father, Augustine Gerard Bou left this bodily life. He was a man of great strength, who had been a farmer, and his native land was Holland.

On the Feast of St. Calixtus, Pope and Martyr, died Hermann Restikey, a Clerk of the diocese of Cologne; he was born in the town of Kempen, and was well learned and skilled in singing and in binding books. When he drew near to death he asked that a taper might be lighted quickly and given into his hands, and holding this above his breast he began to say devoutly and often to repeat: "Mary, Mother of Grace, Mother of Mercy, do thou protect us from the enemy and receive us in the hour of death," and having said this, he breathed forth his soul.

On the day after the Feast of the Eleven Thousand Holy Virgins, John of Kempen fell asleep in the Lord; he was a devout Clerk of the diocese of Cologne who had just been received into the Religious Order, but he died or ever he could take the habit, for death was beforehand with him. He was kinsman to the aforesaid Hermann, whom he had persuaded to withdraw from the life of the world when he was Sublector in the town of Campen. These greatly loved one another in life and death, they came from one city and province, they were of one heart in their good purpose, and alike steadfast therein. This John, who continued a longer space in the service of God, was a man of great kindliness and sobriety, and was well skilled in the work of husbandry. For at harvest time when all must labour more than usual he was diligent in helping therein. And sometimes at night he would gather in the crops of the poor, and often wearied himself by this work of piety; but in this year the weather was very rainy, and the crops were in such danger that he gathered in those that grew in the watery places, and binding them into sheaves carried them on his own shoulders out of reach of the waters.

On the Feast Day of the Saints Crispin and Crispian died Wichbold, son of John of Deventer, a man of good lineage. For a long time he lived a devout life in Zwolle, but afterward finished his days yet more devoutly on the Mount. Being an eager lover of the Scriptures he edified many by his holy discourse. On the Feast Day of St. Martin the Confessor, Henry of Deventer fell asleep in Christ; he was a Clerk and the companion and fellow citizen of Wichbold, and likewise a very humble and gentle man. One day he was plastering the inner walls of the cells in the dormitory of the Brotherhood with soft mortar in company with another Clerk. But it happened that as the mortar was somewhat violently dashed on to the wall some did come through the cracks of the battens into Henry's face (for he was standing on the other side of the wall) and befouled him greatly. But he who had done the deed, looking to see who had been bespattered by the mortar, and seeing the Brother who was so greatly loved with his face befouled, implored his pardon in dolorous wise. But Henry was rather merry than vexed, and answered: "There is no hurt done, be not disturbed. I care not for it." So gentle was he that none ever saw him angered or heard him complain.

The day after the Feast of Brixius, Confessor and Bishop, died Hermann of Laer, a man of great age who came from Campen.

On the Vigil of St. Thomas the Apostle, died Gerlac ten Water, a Clerk of the town of Kampen. He had a deep devotion to the Blessed Virgin, and was still in the flower of his youth, but in this same year he left the world and his parents and entered the monastery with joy, and he made a good end to his life when came the time appointed for him to die. These were buried in the Chapel of St. Agnes, which afterward became the Chapter House, because there was no other consecrated ground in the which they could be buried. But as the space was very narrow, some were buried in a neighbouring spot, because it was hoped that a burial-ground would soon be consecrated there.

But in the year 1407, in the time of William Vorniken, the second Prior, and after the consecration of the new chapel, the bones of some of these Brothers were taken up and buried again in the other burial-ground on the western side of the chapel, where now several Lay Brothers who knew them lie buried also.

In the same year, on the Feast day of St. Martin, the Bishop, Brother Egbert Linghen, the first Rector, invested two converts; their names being Brother John, son of James of Hasselt, and Brother John Eme of Zwolle.

In the year 1399, on the Feast of St. Gregory the Pope, Brother Godefried of Kempen, who was born in the diocese of Cologne, was invested by the first Rector. He was a skilful writer and singer, and he wrote one missal for the High Altar, and three Antiphonaries, and likewise illuminated several books. Also he painted and adorned the altars of the church most beautifully with the figures of saints.

CHAPTER VIII.

How John Kempen was chosen as the first Prior of Mount St. Agnes.

In the year 1399, after Easter, John of Kempen, one of the community at Windesem, was chosen to be Prior of the House of Mount St. Agnes.

By the help of God, he, the first Prior, did govern the affairs of the House, with the many poor inmates, zealously and devoutly for nine years. Also he added to the possessions of the monastery in laudable wise, providing buildings and books and other things needful. He it was that ordered the building of the chief part of the church walls, and he made ready much timber for the finishing of the roof. He began to plant an orchard on the south side of the cloister, and he set forest trees round it on every side. This is that very garden that Gerard Groote, long before, pointed out to the Brothers that they should grow their herbs therein. For a long time wheat was grown, but a great while after herbs were planted.

In the days of the Prior, mountains and hills were made low, and hollow valleys were filled up: then was fulfilled to the letter that which is written in Esaias, a text oft spoken of by the Brothers in the midst of their toil: "Every valley shall be filled and every mountain and hill shall be made low, and the crooked shall be made straight and the rough ways plain" . . .

It is no easy task to tell with what toil and sweat this mountainous place was turned into a level plane, and this sandy soil made abundantly fruitful. Very heavy and long was the labour of preparing a site for the burial-ground and church, for here the slope was steeper than in other places, and extended over the whole face of the ground. Yet by little and little and by labour done at divers times this hill was taken away and the matter thereof thrown outside the boundary wall into a deep valley toward the north: so that to the wonder of many scarce a trace of the said hill could be seen. And the Brothers who worked by turns there would say to one another: "True is the word of the Lord which He spake: 'If ye have faith as a grain of mustard seed ye shall say to this mountain, be thou removed from hence hither and it shall be done!' But since faith without works is dead, we do firmly believe that if we put our hand to this work in the name of the Lord, we shall quickly remove this mountain." So it was done, not to this mountain only but also to others that stood round about the monastery when the boundaries thereof began to be enlarged and to be surrounded by a wall of stone. Besides this Prior John set up the following needful buildings: namely, a Refectory for the Brothers and another for the Lay Folk, a kitchen and cellar, and cells for guests, also a sacristy for Divine service between the choir and the Chapter House. And he himself was the first among them that laboured, and would carry the hod of mortar, and dig with the spade and throw the earth into the cart. When he had leisure he was instant in reading holy books, and often worked at writing or illuminating. He caused several books to be written for the choir and the library, and because they were poor he appointed certain Brothers to write for sale, as was the custom from old time. This many of the Brothers were zealous to do, but others set themselves manfully to the tasks without.

In the year 1399, Indulgences were granted to the people of Zwolle by the Apostolic See, and Pope Boniface the Ninth granted these to be gained by all that were truly penitent at the Church of St. Michael on the Feast of the Finding of the Holy Cross, and on the Feast of St. Michael.

In this same year, I, Thomas of Kempen, a scholar at Deventer and a native of the diocese of Cologne, came to Zwolle to gain indulgences. Then I went on, glad at heart, to Mount St. Agnes, and was instant to be allowed there to abide, and I was received with mercy. Afterward, on the day before the Feast of St. Barbara the Virgin, came William, son of Henry of Amsterdam, who also, at that time, lived at Deventer with the devout Clerks.

CHAPTER IX.

How the Burial-ground at Mount St. Agnes was consecrated.

In the same year, 1399, after the Feast of St. Remigius, the Prior and Brothers of our House took counsel and aid from their friends, and busied themselves about the consecration of the burial-ground, which ceremony had been delayed for a long while because of the hindrances above named. But when they knew that our Lord of Utrecht had returned from the Curia at Rome they came to him in Wollenhoven, where he then lived, and readily obtained their petition through the mediation of their most trusty friends, the noble Sweder of Rechteren and the priest Henry de Ligno.

So that Bishop Frederic, our most kindly lord, delayed not to send to his Suffragan bidding him to come with all speed and consecrate the burial-ground on the Mount, and the Suffragan also when he had read the letter of his Superior was found eager to perform this pious act; and he came without delay with the messengers who had been sent to him, and on the day after the Feast of the Eleven Thousand Virgins, and at about the hour of Vespers, he consecrated the burial-ground that lieth within the cloister of the monastery, the Prior, Brothers, Clerks, and servants of our House being present at the ceremony. When the rite had been performed duly, a gentle rain fell and watered the consecrated ground with the dew of heaven, and all that dwelt thereabout rejoiced with great joy, for that the place had been consecrated by the Bishop, and that the mouths of the adversaries who strove to hinder the foundation and progress of the monastery were evidently stopped.

So when the rite of consecration had been performed by the authority of the Bishop, he went himself on another day to Windesem and there consecrated the new choir and the four altars.

CHAPTER X.

Of the Brothers who were invested by John of Kempen, the first Prior.

In the days of this venerable man our first Prior and Father, seven Clerks and three Converts were invested, and the day and year of their investiture are written below. Likewise he received the profession of Brother Godefried of Kempen who was then about twenty years of age.

In the year of the Lord 1401, on the day after the Dispersion of the Apostles, was invested Brother John Drick of the city of Steenwyck in the diocese of Utrecht. He was before a priest, and Vicar of Steenwyck, and after less than a year of probation he made his profession by licence of the Prior of the Superior House, on the birthday of St. John the Apostle; and he afterward was chosen Procurator.

In the same year, on the Feast day of St. Brixius, Bishop and Confessor, was invested William, son of Henry (who was called William Coman) of Amsterdam in the State of Holland. He was now twenty-three years of age and had lived with the devout Brothers at Deventer, but Florentius Radewin, before his death, sent him to Mount St. Agnes.

In the same year, on the day before the Feast of St. Catherine the Virgin, was invested Brother Frederic, a Convert who was born in Groninghen in the State of Frisia, and lived for a long while on Mount St. Agnes with the first founders of the monastery.

In the year of the Lord 1402, on the Vigil of the Nativity of Christ, was invested Brother Gerard, son of Tydeman, who was born in Wesep, a town in Holland: he wrote divers works for the use of the monastery and for sale. In the year of the Lord 1403, on the day of St. Pontianus the Martyr, was invested Conrad, a Convert; he was a tailor and was born in the Countship of Marck.

In the year of the Lord 1405, on the Festival of the Four Crowned Martyrs, Brother Alardus, a priest, and John Benevolt of

Groninghen were alike invested: Alardus was forty-six years old and a Frisian by nation; he had been Curate at Pilsum, which was his native place, and was a good and devout man.

In the year of the Lord 1406, on the Feast of Corpus Christi, which fell in that year on the day before the Feast of St. Barnabas, two brothers that were Clerks, and one that was a Convert, were invested. These were Thomas Hemerken of the city of Kempen in the diocese of Cologne, and own brother to John of Kempen the first Prior. The father of these was called John and their mother Gertrude. The other Clerk was called Oetbert Wilde of Zwolle, whose father's name was Henry and his mother's Margaret. The Convert was Arnold Droem of Utrecht who brought great wealth to the monastery and was in charge of the Refectory.

CHAPTER XI.

Of the death of Brother Wolfard, Priest in the Monastery of Mount St. Agnes.

In the year of the Lord 1401, on the Feast of the Holy Martyrs John and Paul, Brother Wolfard, son of Matthias, died in the monastery pertaining to our order, which is called the House of the Blessed Virgin in the Wood, and lieth near Northorn. He came from Medenblic, a town in Holland, and was one of the four first Brothers of our House. He was a man of great stature and grave deportment, eloquent in discourse, and his hoary head was comely to look upon. He took part in the labours of the younger Brothers, and would perform lowly tasks, such as washing the trenchers, digging the ground, carrying stones, or collecting wood. It was his wont to come early into the choir, to be alert in watching, enduring in fasting, careful in celebrating the Mass, and devout in prayer. Once he was asked by a Religious what he had eaten during Advent, and whether he had had eggs from time to time; and he made answer: "Blessed be God, throughout Advent I have seldom taken eggs or fish, but I have eaten pulse only and have kept the fast in great contentment."

So when by the ordinance of God the end of his life was at hand, and the time when his good deeds should receive a better crown, he made a most edifying end after the manner and order following:

At that time and in this year there was a notable pestilence in our House of the Blessed Virgin in the Wood, whereof the Prior and many Brothers died, and the one priest who survived, Brother John of Groninghen, a weakly and feeble man, was left desolate save for the presence of one novice, Brother Honestus. But our Brother Wolfard, hearing of the death of these Brothers, and of the grief of them that were left desolate, was greatly moved with compassion for this House. One day, therefore, when girt for labour, he said in a tone of pity to me, as I stood by him, "Who could deserve to have his portion with these good Brothers of Northorn, and to earn an end like theirs?" For he had known divers of these Brothers, and the place where they dwelt, and he loved their holy company. And as he was telling me many good things concerning them, Brother Arnold, a Convert from Northorn, entered in at the gate of our monastery to ask for one of our priests and when Brother Wolfard saw him coming he ran joyfully towards him and embraced him. But hearing the cause of his coming, he said that he himself was ready to go with him if it were pleasing to the Prior, and his obedience should permit. And Arnold, seeing his readiness to come, rejoiced thereat, and said: "Most beloved Brother, how good would it be that thou shouldest do so." Then the Brothers were called together and considered who should be sent to succour those Brothers in their strait, and they determined upon Brother Wolfard, who was of fitting character and age, and he, being moved by charity, assented to their resolution. On the next day at sunrise, he set forth to Northorn with Brother Arnold, being ready to lay down his life for the Brothers after the example of Christ, that he might save it everlastingly. So he said farewell to the Brothers of Mount St. Agnes, who wept at his departure, and left the monastery never to return thither; but he knew not how soon he should be removed to a Higher Mount. In thus leaving the place and the Brothers he overcame his natural man and fulfilled the law of charity, following, in his death, the example of Christ. Therefore he entered into the Monastery of Mary, Mother of Christ, which is in the Wood, and within a few days he there made an end of his life, and was buried by the Brothers of the House aforesaid. Our Brother Egbert hath told me that long ago Gerard Groote had said to our brother: "Wolfard, thou shalt know two conversions," for in the days of Master Gerard, Wolfard had begun to be well disposed to the religious life, but afterward he was turned away to the world: yet after many years, by the grace of God, it came about that he was again pricked to the heart, and, leaving his pastoral charge, he changed his worldly life, and was among the first of the Brothers to take the religious habit, and he thus ended his life with a happy death struggle.

CHAPTER XII.

How Brother William Forniken was chosen to be the second Prior in the House of Mount St. Agnes.

In the year of the Lord 1408, on the Vigil of Ascension Day, Brother William Vorniken, from the Monastery at Windesem, was chosen to be Prior of Mount St. Agnes. He was the second Prior of our House, which he ruled for seventeen years, being a lover of poverty and discipline. After that he was taken away from us he was promoted to the Superior House at Windesem, and became Father General of all our Order. He it was who looked to the roofing of the church, the making of new stalls in the choir, and the provision of fair vestments to be worn by priests and servers on festivals. Also he enlarged the borders of the monastery, and surrounded the whole with a wall of stone; he built a new dwelling for the husbandmen and placed a byre for cattle near the gate, likewise in the year of his departure he began to make a mill and to build a brewery. In several places he planted trees of divers kinds, of which some were fruit trees; and he made smooth the slopes of the mountain, which for the most part still remained steep, and this he did by carrying away the sandy soil.

He ordered the altars to be beautified with pictures, and good store of books to be written for the choir and the library. Yet in the midst of all these things poverty and simplicity were dear to him, and with his own hand he illuminated many books. He took divers Lay Brothers to dwell with him, for he saw with the eye of charity that they would earn the reward of eternal life by faithfully cleaving to their holy labours, and living the common life under obedience. Some of these he received as Donates, others he invested with the habit of Converts.

During the years that he was Prior he invested fourteen Clerks, whose names, with the days of their investiture, are written hereafter.

In the year 1408, on the Feast of St. Michael the Archangel, was invested Brother Nicholas Creyenschot, a native of the town of Kampen, a youth in years but upright in character.

In the year 1410, on the Feast of All Saints, two Brothers were invested together, namely, Wermbold, a priest of Kampen and kinsman to John of Ummen, and Gerard Ae of Utrecht.

In the year 1411, on the Vigil of the Nativity, three Brothers were invested together, namely, John the son of Gerard, John Bowman, and Gerard son of Wolter, a Convert; all these came from Zwolle. In the year 1413, on the Feast of the Visitation of the Blessed Virgin, was invested Brother John of Lent, a town one mile from Zwolle. In the year 1418, on the Vigil of the Nativity, three Brothers were invested together, namely, Rudolph of Oetmersen in Twenthe, Otto Lyman of Goch in Geldria, and Henry the son of James of Zwolle.

In the year 1421, on the Vigil of the Nativity, two Brothers were invested: namely, Henry, son of William, of Deventer, and Deric Veneman of Zwolle.

In the year 1423, on Easter Eve, two Converts were invested, namely, Gerard ten Mollen of Zwolle, and Gerard Hombolt of Utrecht.

In the year of the Lord 1424, on the Feast of the Annunciation of the Blessed Virgin Mary, these three Brothers were invested: John Lap of the town of Neerden in Holland, Christian Anversteghe of Campen, and Helmic Braem of Herderwijck in the State of Geldria.

CHAPTER XIII.

Of the death of Brother Nicholas Kreyenschot.

In the year 1410, on the Feast of St. Barnabas the Apostle, Nicholas Kreyenschot died just after sunset. He was a youth of good disposition, and sprang from a notable family of the town of Kampen. He was about twenty-three years of age, for God dealt pitifully with him so that his short span of life fulfilled the task of many years, and he escaped longer struggles in this present life; for eight months and ten days after his profession he left dwelling in this present world and departed to the other. The virtue of obedience shone brightly in him, as was seemly in a good youth. Who should say, "Brother, come hither," and Nicholas would not come straightway, or "Begone," and he did not straightway depart? Moreover, a good return came to the monastery through his means. It happened in a time that he upset and broke a jar, and so grieved was he at this mischance and loss, that he wept bitterly. Once also he made ready a sharp rod, and came to the sub-Prior, saying: "I entreat thee, Father, for God's sake, to inflict a sharp discipline upon me, for I do often transgress, nor do I make any progress." He was buried in the eastern part of the cloister near the wall of the church and beneath the steps of our dormitory.

CHAPTER XIV.

Of the consecration of our Church and of four Altars in the House of Mount St. Agnes.

In the year 1412, on the 8th day of the month of April, being the Friday after Easter, our church was consecrated, being dedicated in honour of St. Agnes the Virgin and Martyr of Christ. The rite was performed by Matthias of Biduane, the Suffragan of our Lord and Reverend Father in Christ, Frederic de Blanckenhem, Bishop of Utrecht. Many religious persons and priests were present thereat, namely, the Prior of Windesem, the Prior of Belheem, Conrad Hengel and John of Haarlem, who were priests at Zwolle. Many other honourable persons also, both men and women, young and old, men of the town and men of the country, came together to this dedication. There was great joy in the hearts of all, and a general license to enter the monastery was given to strangers, as our statutes allow to be done on that day only. So when the consecration had been solemnly performed, the Bishop came forward in his mitre to consecrate the four altars. First he dedicated the High Altar in the Choir in honour of the Holy Trinity, the Blessed Mother of God, St. Agnes the Virgin, and the Apostles of Christ, and he sang Mass in solemn wise for the dedication of the church and altar.

Then going out of the Choir into the northern aisle of the church, he dedicated the Altar in the greater chapel in honour of the Holy Cross and the Blessed Martyrs, and afterwards the Altar which is in the midst of the church on the left of the Choir in honour of the Blessed Mary ever Virgin, and of St. Augustine the Bishop, who is Father of our Order.

Lastly, he dedicated the Altar on the south side of the Choir in honour of the most Blessed Mary Magdalene, St. Catherine, St. Cecilia, and the Eleven Thousand Virgins.

This done, masses were celebrated at the several altars, and the Host of Salvation was offered up in all reverence to God. But after midday, the Brothers being gathered together, he consecrated the burial-ground for the interment of the dead outside the church and on the western and southern side thereof.

On that day he granted Indulgences for forty days to them that were there present, and a like grace to all the benefactors of the church and all that visited the altars, as was set forth clearly in the Bishop's letter concerning the consecration of the church. In this same church there still stand the two altars that were consecrated in Westerhof at the first foundation of the House in that place; for these, by consent of the Bishop of Utrecht, were transferred to this church after the return of the Brothers from Westerhof. One of these was consecrated in honour of St. John the Baptist and the Blessed Apostles St. Peter and St. Paul; this doth stand on the south side of the church. The other was dedicated in honour of St. James and St. John the Apostles.

The Sunday after the Feast of the Blessed Gallus the Abbot (which is in the month of October), was appointed to be kept in every year as the anniversary of the dedication of this church and the several altars therein; and on this day also is kept the Dedication Festival of the House of the Blessed Virgin in Windesem and of the Convent of Nuns at Diepenveen, to the glory and honour of the most Blessed Trinity.

In the same year, when their General Chapter was held at Windesem, the venerable Fathers of the Canons Regular in Brabant came thereto, and were accepted and united to our Fraternity, together with the Houses belonging to them.

In this year from the Feast of Pentecost onward the Canonical Hours were sung in our church after the monastic manner.

CHAPTER XV.

Of the death of the beloved Father John Ummen, the first Founder of the Monastery of Mount St. Agnes.

In the year 1420, in the evening of the 1st day of September, the Feast of St. Ægidius the Abbot, died that holy and faithful servant of Christ, John Reghelant, formerly a most beloved disciple of Gerard Groote, whose discourses he used to hear. He was born of honest parents, and for several years was educated in Zwolle; but while he was yet a youth he was diseased in the eyes, and God allowed him to fall into darkness, and he continued blind to the end of his life; but yet the less he could see the outer world, the more brightly did the grace of God illumine him inwardly. His mother, whose name was Regheland, was devoted to God, and often went on long journeys to visit the shrines of Saints in company with her blind son, whom she would lead by the hand, taking him with her to hear sermons in church, and leading him onward to every good thing.

So when the venerable Master, Gerard Groote, was preaching in Zwolle, and through God's inspiration was bringing compunction to many, the Lord did open the heart of this His servant also, and did inflame him, wherefore he began to love Gerard much, and often sought to be instructed by the doctrine of so great a man. For this cause he left wandering about the world and sought to serve God in quietness, also he exhorted all that came to him to despise earthly desires, and take hold on that new life in Christ which Gerard taught by his holy manner of living.

Therefore he took to him certain men that were well disposed, and with them he began to live the Common Life in Zwolle, but afterward they took up their abode upon Mount Nemel (which is now called Mount St. Agnes), because they wished to dwell outside the tumult of the world. Here they gathered a larger company, the which he governed for many years with faithful devotion, assisted by divers helpers, until the monastery was founded, for he did not fear the many hindrances that met him. But at length when the monastery was builded, and a Prior instituted in the canonical manner, John, being filled with brotherly love, and led by a yet fuller zeal for souls, took with him certain laymen of ripe age and began to form a new congregation in honour of the Holy Trinity, in the field of St. John, near Vollenhoe, which congregation, by the favour of God, he did enlarge greatly. And when in the process of time the number of the Brothers was multiplied, he and many others took the habit of the Tertiaries, and he continued to his life's end to be the humble servant of the Brothers and their first Rector. He was one of the first and original disciples of Gerard Groote, and had many spiritual discourses with him, for it was from Gerard that he learned the way of an holy life, and he submitted himself and his little ones fully to Gerard's counsel and discretion. Being prevented in due season by God's grace, Father John was devout, and is worthy of remembrance, for that going on day by day he reached forward continually to the things that are before, being a notable lover of poverty, one that kept lowliness and loved sobriety. He was the very beauty of purity, a pattern of simplicity, a strong upholder of discipline, an enemy of sin, a light of virtue, an ensample of devotion, strong in faith, long suffering in hope, prodigal in charity, and one that did convert many from the vanity of the world. A few things concerning him are written in the beginning of this book.

So being wearied by his many years, when the day of his release from captivity was nigh, and he was dwelling in the house of the Sisters at Almelo, he fell sick; and having fulfilled seventy years of life, he fell asleep in the Lord and was buried in the chapel of the Sisterhood there. After his happy departure, John of Resa, a devout priest, was chosen as the second minister of the House of St. John, and he sought and obtained for that House certain privileges that were needful, and also the consecration of the burial-ground, which things were granted by the Venerable Frederic, Lord Bishop of Utrecht. After him Christian, a native of Zeeland, and one that had made his profession, was chosen as priest to that House, and was the third to administer and rule the same.

CHAPTER XVI.

Of the pestilence that afflicted mankind, and how some of our Brothers died in this plague.

In the year 1421 there was a notable pestilence in Deventer, Zwolle, Kampen, and the neighbouring towns, and during the three months of summer much people of the land were slain thereby. In the same year, after the Feast of the Nativity of St. John the Baptist, the Cross was preached against the heretics of Prague, who stirred up a grievous persecution against Holy Church, the clergy, and the Christian people; and led away many faithful persons by threatenings and deceits: likewise they destroyed monasteries and churches, and put many persons to a cruel death. In the same year in the month of September the disease laid hold on certain of our household, for the pestilence did mightily increase, and on the Octave of the Nativity of the Virgin Mary, after High Mass, a Lay Brother named Nicholas died. He was born in Drenthe, and had been our miller, a man of good reputation and life, and well beloved by all that were in the House.

On the Feast of St. Lambert, Bishop and Martyr, and about the hour of Vespers, died our Brother Oetbert Wilde, a fervent and devout priest. The Brothers were with him when he died, and they offered up prayers after the accustomed manner. He was in the thirty-eighth year of his age, and the fifteenth after his profession: he came from Zwolle, where he was born of very honest parents, and he loved our patroness St. Agnes the Virgin with a special devotion. In the beginning he suffered many weaknesses and temptations, but afterward, by the help of God, he was changed into another man, mightily uplifted from pusillanimity of spirit, and endowed with much grace of devotion. He died happily after a good struggle, and on the next day his body was buried next to Brother Nicholas Kreyenschot on the eastern side of the cloister, and Mass and prayers were said for him.

On the Feast of St. Michael, after Vespers had been said, Nicholas, son of Peter, departed this life. He was a Donate of our House, and a carpenter, being a man of great stature and mighty strength, and he had lived for more than twenty years in the House of Mount St. Agnes. He came from Monekedam in Holland, and having lived with us from the very beginning of the monastery, he left a good memorial of his skill and industry in his craft in the building of the church, and the new stalls for the Brothers in the choir. His body was laid in the burial-ground of the Laics, toward the south part and near the path.

On the day of St. Jerome the Priest, at about the time when the midday meal was ended, died Riquin of Urdinghen, a Donate of our House who attended the sick. He departed after a brief agony, while Litanies were sung round his death-bed: his native place was in the diocese of Cologne, and during the twenty-five years that he lived in the House on the Mount he never visited his friends, nor saw his native land once he had departed from her. He loved the Blessed Virgin with singleness of heart, and on the seventh day of the week he abstained from one portion of pottage out of devotion to her. In these three desires he was heard of the Lord before his death, namely, to die on an high day, and amid the Brothers—for he greatly loved them—and to have a short death struggle; which things were so brought to pass by our good Lord even as he had desired them out of his good and simple heart.

On the Feast Day of St. Luke the Evangelist, at about the fifth hour of the morning, died Adam of Herderwijck, a Donate of our House, who had sojourned in this place for twenty years. He submitted himself to divers toils and discommodities by his devotion and faithfulness to the business of the House; he was pitiful to the poor, kindly to the afflicted, and in this time of stress he ministered with care and diligence to the Brothers that were sick. His body was laid in the burying ground of the Laics near the other Donates, and after his burial the pestilence was stayed, for God had pity on us, and some that had been smitten by this stroke grew whole of their disease.

In this year, after the Feast of All Saints, Brother Gerard Ae, once an inmate of the House on the Mount, died in Frisia in the Convent of the Nuns at Berghen.

In the same year, on the Feast of St. Lucia the Virgin, Peter Valkenburrigh the Priest departed this life. He had lived an humble life for a long while with the Brothers in the Field of St. John near Vollenhoe, and he desired to be buried upon Mount St. Agnes, where he had dwelt in former days, with the first Brothers of the House; for they of the Field of St. John had not as yet a consecrated burying ground; so he was laid to rest on the eastern side of ours next to Winald the Priest, who was once chaplain to our Lord Frederic, Bishop of Utrecht, and a friend to the Brothers on the Mount.

CHAPTER XVII.

Of the death of William, son of Seger, a Priest in Hasselt.

In the year of the Lord 1422, on the Vigil of Ascension Day, which was the day following the Feast of St. Potentiana, died that devout priest, William, son of Seger, the Confessor of the Sisters of the Third Order at Hasselt. He was born in Zwolle, and was buried, as he had long desired, on the eastern side of the precinct before the Prior's Cell. There were present at his burial these venerable men, namely, Father Wessel, first Superior of Kleerwater, near Hattem, Father John Haerlem, Confessor of the Sisters at Zwolle, Father Gerard Trecht, and Father Stephen Mulart, who were priests in Hasselt. Also many other honourable men, and friends of the said William, came together to his burial from the aforesaid towns, and the Prior of the House recited the burial office with faithful devotion in presence of the Brothers.

After his death Father Gerard Trecht was called by the Fathers of our Order to rule over the aforesaid Sisters in the room of the departed Brother.

In the same year, during the days of Pentecost, peace was established between the men of Utrecht and Holland, and those of Geldria, for during a whole year they had been at grievous enmity, and many deeds of rapine, murder, and arson had been wrought in evil wise on both sides.

In the month of September, on the day before the Feast of S. S. Cosmas and Damianus, Brother John Pric, a priest and inmate of the House of Mount St. Agnes, died in Thabor in Frisia. He was born in the town of Steenwyck, and had been Vicar of the Church of St. Clement in that place, but after several years, at the request of the Prior at Thabor, he dwelt for a time with the Brothers of that House, and in the same year many died in the pestilence, amongst whom he also fell asleep in the Lord, and was buried with the other Brothers in that place on the eastern side of the cloister. This was his motto for the novices: "He that doth not accustom himself to exercises of humility at the beginning of his conversion, and doth not break down his own will, shall seldom become a good Religious."

In the month of October, on the day of the translation of St. Augustine the Bishop, there died at Zwolle that honourable dame, Mary, the widow of Henry de Haerst, our neighbour. She was truly pious and pitiful towards the needy, and often came humbly to Mount St. Agnes to hear the Holy Offices. Moreover, she abstained from all wordly adornments in her vesture, and she left a good bequest to our Brotherhood on the Mount, where also she doth lie buried in the church in the same tomb with Bartold her son.

In the year 1423 there was such mighty cold and frost that endured from Epiphany even to the Feast of St. Peter's Chair at Antioch, that the hardness of the frost brought great masses of ice across the waters. Wherefore at the beginning of March, when the snow and ice melted suddenly in the heat of the sun, a great flood of waters followed, and the dykes were burst by the rushing thereof, so that much of the corn land was overflowed, and the seeds perished.

In the summer of the same year the boundary wall round our monastery was finished even from the south to the western side, and a new gate was made.

In this same year, on Easter Eve, two Converts were invested, namely, Brother Gerard ten Mollen, and Brother Gerard Hombolt, as is recorded above.

CHAPTER XVIII.

Of the death of our most reverend Lord Frederic, Bishop of Utrecht.

In the year of the Lord 1423, on the Feast Day of S. Dionysius, Bishop and Martyr, which is the ninth day of October, that most reverend and renowned Lord Frederic of Blankenhem, the illustrious Bishop of Utrecht, went away out of the light of this world, being about eighty years of age.

He ruled the diocese of Utrecht strenuously and in honourable wise during thirty years, for the grace of God Almighty succoured him: his power was increased by many victories, and he gave the Church peace, his country safety, and his people tranquillity before his death. This is he that was a potentate of renown, a pillar of the priesthood, a guiding star to Clerks, a father to the Religious, a friend to all devout persons, a defender of the orphan, an avenger upon the unjust.

This is he that was the glory of rulers, the delight of subjects, that upheld dignity among the aged, and uprightness amongst the young, he was a pinnacle of learning, the ornament of the wise; he gave weapons to the warriors and a shield to them that strove: he inspired terror in his foes, and courage in his people; he was an ornament to the nobles, an honour to princes, a glory to the great ones of the land. Who could tell his praises in worthy wise, for in his days all was well ordered in the land of Utrecht! Prelates were honest, and priests pious in the worship of God; the religious were devout, the virgins were chaste, the people were fervent in the faith, judges were firm, and wealth grew abundantly in the cities. In these days also, schools for learning flourished, especially at Deventer and Zwolle, and a vast multitude of learners came together from divers states and regions, both near and afar off. And because the Bishop feared God, honoured Holy Church, and loved and defended all that served the Lord, therefore the Majesty on High protected him from the enemies that were round about, making rebellious nations subject to him, especially those Frisians who had invaded his territories. Moreover, God did make his days illustrious by many marvellous deeds, so that an age of gold seemed to have been granted to his land of Utrecht. But this did appear more evidently after the Bishop's death, when a schism—exceeding lawless and long enduring—arose and increased among Clerks and people alike. And this the reverend Bishop feared should come about, for he was a prudent man and a learned; moreover, he knew the manners of the cities and the seditious ways of some of the nobles whose insolence he had been able to restrain and subdue with difficulty, and the exercise of great valour. "After my death," said he, "they will know that they have had a good lord, for they all wish to be masters, and to have none set over them, wherefore it shall be ill with them." And he prophesied truly, for the whole land of Utrecht suffered grievous loss for her sedition, and shall long mourn the same, as will be shown briefly in the proper place.

So this illustrious ruler died in his castle that is called Horst, not far from Utrecht, and his body was brought by a seemly train of followers to the church at Utrecht where his predecessors were buried, and there in company with the other bishops in an honoured tomb upon the right side of the choir he doth rest in peace.

CHAPTER XIX.

Of the death of Brother John Vos of Huesden, who was the second Prior at Windesem.

In the year of the Lord 1424, on the Saturday following the Feast of St. Andrew, being the second of December, the venerable Father John Huesden, who was the second Prior of Windesem, died in the sixty-first year of his age. He had been a disciple of Master Gerard Groote and Father Florentius, Vicar of Deventer, and on the Feast of St. Mary Magdalene, in the year following the investiture of the first Brothers, he himself was invested there together with Henry Balveren. A short time after Brother Werner, the first Prior, was absolved from his office, this John Huesden was chosen the second Prior of the House, being then in the twenty-eighth year of his age. By the help of God he continued as Prior for thirty-three years and ruled the House in a laudable manner: also he was of much profit to the whole Order, being a most comfortable and kindly Father to all the devout Brothers and Sisters that were in the whole Diocese, for he was charitably disposed to all alike. He ordered the writing of many books for the monastery, being a fervent lover of the holy writings, and was specially devoted to our Father Saint Augustine, a store of whose books he collected diligently. He was also at Constance in the days of the General Council, whither he went in company with John Wale, the venerable Prior of Zwolle, and the cardinals and other prelates received them both kindly and with reverence.

Now it came to pass a few days before his death, and within the Octave of St. Martin the Bishop, that two Brothers came from Mount St. Agnes to Windesem to commune with the Prior. And one of them had a dream after this wise, which vision did foretell the Prior's death; for he saw the spirits gathered together in Heaven and hastening as if to the death-bed of some one, and straightway he heard a bell toll as if for the passing of a dying man, and the sound hereof aroused him, and he awoke. So rising from his bed and desiring to go to see what had happened, he perceived no man, for it was before the fifth hour in the morning, and the Brothers were yet asleep. So, returning to himself, he kept silence, and the thought came to him that our Father the Prior should soon depart hence. Yet he told naught of this vision to any that were in the House, but to a certain Clerk that was coming from Brabant and journeying in his company he said privately: "Tell Hermann Scutken, who sojourneth at Thenen, to come quickly if he would speak with our Father at Windesem, for if the vision that one hath seen this night is true, I wot that he shall not long abide here." So when fifteen days were passed this Reverend Father died on the day aforesaid after High Mass, and before the midday meal the Mass of the dead was sung for him, and his body was buried in the choir before the step of the sanctuary.

On the Vigil of the Epiphany after the death of this venerable Father, Brother Gerard Naeldwijc, the Procurator of the House, was chosen to be Prior; but he was greatly grieved thereat, and after a long while he consented, though against his will. Being lowly and gentle he might not bear the honour and burden of this place, and he sought earnestly with many prayers to be relieved from the care of so great a charge, and when the next General Chapter was held he sought to be absolved from his office of Prior, which petition was granted to him. So after he had been absolved, and when the Fathers were still gathered together, Brother William Vorniken, the Prior of Mount St. Agnes, was chosen by the same General Chapter to be Prior of the Superior House. And when he knew of his election he too was stricken with dismay, for he was afraid of the burden, which is indeed a thing to fear. So he wept abundantly, saying again and again that he was unworthy, and striving mightily against this thing in every manner, yet was he obliged to obey and to take upon himself for Christ's sake the yoke of so great a burden, being compelled thereto by his obedience and the determination of the more part. Therefore, at length, he consented, and after weeping bitterly he was confirmed and inducted into the office, and all that were in the House gave thanks to God and were glad; but the House of Mount St. Agnes was saddened above measure and wept when her faithful Pastor was taken from her, for she knew none like to him.

CHAPTER XX.

How Brother Theodoric of Kleef was chosen to be the third Prior of the House on the Mount.

In the year of the Lord 1425, the House of Mount St. Agnes bereft of her Pastor (who had been chosen for and translated to the Superior House) was instant to provide for herself another suitable ruler in accordance with the canons. Wherefore the Brothers were gathered together, and on the Saturday after Pentecost the Mass of the Holy Spirit was celebrated after the monastic manner, and all the members of the Chapter came together to the Chapter House. When the opinion of each had been heard, Brother Theodoric of Kleef, our Sub-Prior, was chosen, and those venerable Fathers, the Prior of Windesem and the Prior of the House of the Blessed Virgin, near Northorn, took part in this election, and confirmed the same as an holy act by the authority committed to them.

Brother Theodoric was one of the elder Brothers of this same House, and had been among those that were first invested: he had a long training in the good life, and he wrote summer and winter Homilies together with certain other books.

After his election as Father and third Prior of our House, many evils befel in the diocese of Utrecht, which same did mightily afflict our House and all the devout in the land. This was by reason of a schism between Sueder of Culenborgh, who was confirmed as Bishop of the diocese, and the noble Rodolph of Diepholt, and the long continued strife between these two did disturb many Clerks and citizens of the land.

In the same year, on the Feast of the Visitation of the Blessed Virgin Mary, and after Compline, died our Brother Conrad, a Convert. He was the tailor, and was born in Scyrebeke in the Countship of Marck, and had lived at Deventer under Florentius, which devout Father sent him to Mount St. Agnes when he had learned the tailor's art. He lived devoutly and humbly with us for many years, making, cleaning, and mending the raiment of the Brothers, but toward the end of his life it was his chief delight to think that he had often cleansed their clothing, for he hoped by his labours in this regard to have cleansed also the stains of his own sins. He was a man right pure and modest, and one that loved poverty and simplicity, and he ardently longed to be released and to be with Christ Jesus and Mary, whom he often called upon by name at the last: moreover, it was given him to die a peaceful and an holy death on this day of Her Festival, and his body was laid in the burying ground within the cloister of the monastery, hard by the northern gate, toward the wall of the eastern building. In the same year Sueder of Culenborgh was confirmed Bishop of Utrecht by the authority of the Apostolic See, and he was accepted by the people of Utrecht, and of certain other towns, but by the States of Overyssel he was not received. Wherefore these States were placed under an Interdict, and a great controversy arose among Clerks and people, for some observed the Interdict, but the chief ones of the States with those that clove to them, clamoured against it.

Alas! Holy God! on the day before the Feast of St. Lambert we ceased from our singing by reason of the Interdict that was published against us! For this cause the nobles of the land and many of the vulgar had indignation against us and other Religious, and we suffered many insults, and at last we were driven to go forth from our country and our monasteries in order to observe the Interdict.

In the same year, on the holy day of Christ's Nativity, were invested two Clerks that had been Probationers a long while, and also one Convert named James Cluit of Kampen who had studied for some time at Deventer under John of Jülich, the famous and devout Rector. The Clerks were Brother Gerard Smullinc of Kleef, who had attended the school at Zwolle under Master John Cele, the excellent Rector with whom he dwelt for some space as a fellow commoner: and Brother James Ae, a Convert from Utrecht, and kinsman to Brother William Vorniken who was once our Prior.

CHAPTER XXI.

Of the death of Brother Egbert formerly Sub-Prior at the House on the Mount.

In the year of the Lord 1427, on the day after the Feast of St. Ægidius the Abbot, and after the third hour of the night, Brother Egbert of Linghen died at Diepenveen in the House of the Sisters of our Order. He was Rector and Confessor of that House, and was buried in the church there, outside the choir and between the two chancels, the Prior of Windesem being present at his burial.

This Brother was born in the town of Ummen and baptised in the church of St. Bridget: but when his parents removed to Zwolle, he being a youth of good disposition began to attend the school under Master John Cele, and earnestly to profit thereby. And when he heard the honourable reputation of the House on the Mount he came thither eagerly: now the elder John Ummen then ruled over it, and his wholesome exhortations touched Egbert to his good, so being now sufficiently advanced in learning he left his parents, and in humility and devotion joined himself to these Brothers—the poor little ones of Christ. Afterward he was promoted to the Priesthood in this same House, and since the grace of devotion grew in him, in a short time he, with two others, took the Religious habit. These three were the first to take it, and Egbert the first amongst them. Also he was for a time Sub-Prior of our House on the Mount, being a man of good heart, eloquent in word, diligent in writing, a comforter of them that sorrowed, quick to forgive injuries, and one that did rejoice with all his heart at the progress of others. He adorned many of the chant books in the choir with beautiful illuminations, and also divers books for our library, and sometimes those that were written for sale. He loved our House on Mount St. Agnes above all places that are on the earth, and he laboured right faithfully for the building thereof. Moreover, when his parents were dead, he, their only son, received all their goods as their lawful heir; and these were given for the common use of the Brothers who had heretofore lived in great lack. Wherefore year by year memorial is made of him and his parents in the monastery for these benefits, as is justly due.

CHAPTER XXII.

How our Brothers and other Religious were driven from the land by reason of the Interdict.

In the year of the Lord 1429, the strife between them that followed Sueder and them that clave to Rodolph—who had been chosen to be Bishop—still continued, and heavy threats were made against the Regulars in that they obeyed the letter of the Apostolic See and the commandments of Sueder, Bishop of Utrecht. And since they would not consent to the appeal of Rodolph, nor maintain his cause, they were driven either to begin again to sing the services of the church or to depart from the country, they and all their company.

Then did the Priors take counsel with their congregations, and they chose rather to give place to the people that were enraged against them, and to be exiles for justice' sake than to consent to such commandments to the scandal of all the devout, for these had already gone away from a great part of the country, leaving their own houses and their native land.

Therefore, when this grievous choice was made known before the Fathers and Brothers of our House, there was but one opinion amongst all, namely, that they must prepare to sojourn in a strange land and so keep obedience to the Apostolic See, but that they should leave in the monastery certain of their household that were Lay Brothers, Converts and Donates, who might keep the House. Thus were the Brothers driven forth, and they departed publicly before sunset on the Feast of St. Barnabas the Apostle. Moreover the Brothers of Windesem with their household went forth toward Northorn, and they of Bethlehem in Zwolle went over the Yssel to the district of Geldria. But the Brothers of Mount St. Agnes abode at Hasselt for the first night, and on the next day they took ship for Frisia meaning to go to their Brothers at Lunenkerc, to help and comfort that House which they had begun to reform. And by the help of God, while many of our Brothers sojourned there, the House soon came to be well ordered. There were together in the hired ship in which they crossed over twenty-four of our household, both Clerks and Lay Brothers, and these abode three years in Lunenkerc for the name of Christ and the Church of God; and the exile from their own land, which they took patiently, bore notable fruit.

These are the names of our Brothers and the others of our household, both Clerks and Laics, who were driven from the land of Utrecht and from our monastery for their obedience in the matter of the Interdict which they observed for more than a year by command of the Apostolic See.

First our venerable Father the Prior, who was called Brother Theodoric of Kleef; the second was Brother Thomas of Kempen, the Sub-Prior; the third, Brother John Ummen, who was stricken in years and weak; the fourth, Brother Gerard Wesep; the fifth, Brother John Benevolt; the sixth, Brother Wernbold Staelwijc; the seventh, Brother John Bouman; the eighth, Brother Henry Cremer; the ninth, Brother Henry of Deventer; the tenth, Brother Dirk Veneman; the eleventh, Brother Helmic; the twelfth, Brother Christian; the thirteenth, Brother James Cluyt; the fourteenth, Brother Gerard Smullinc; the fifteenth, Brother Cesarius, a Novice; the sixteenth, Brother Goswin, son of Pistor, a Novice.

Likewise there were two Converts, namely, Brother Arnold Droem and Brother James Ae; three Clerks that had not yet received the Religious habit, namely, Hermann Craen, Gosswin ten Velde, and Arnold ten Brincke; two Donates named Gerard Hombolt and Laurence, and also John Koyte, a guest and familiar friend of our House. All of these were received for the first night as the guests of the Sisters at Hasselt, who showed great charity and humanity towards us, and they lamented and wept bitterly that we were driven out with violence. But since all the Brothers could not find room nor beds wherein to sleep, these Sisters had compassion upon us and brought us their own bedding wherewith they prepared a place for us to sleep in the stable on the hay and straw, and here we all slept commodiously enough. Many of the citizens in Hasselt also had compassion upon us and wept, but certain envious folk that thought ill of us mocked our Brothers and spake lightly of them, but of these divers did afterward repent. On the second day, when morning came, we hired a small ship and came by way of the sea to Frisia, the land we sought, having taken sustenance by the way; but we used both sails and oars and gat us across not without great hazard for the wind was contrary. Thus we went thither for the name of Christ and to keep obedience to the Holy Roman Church, the which we all desired to obey, and we committed ourselves to God Who showed forth His mercy toward us, and snatching us from the peril of the sea brought us safely to our Brothers in Lunenkerc.

In the year 1430, on the 19th day of December, being the day before the Vigil of St. Thomas the Apostle, died our beloved Brother John, a priest who was born at Kampen. He was third among the first four who received investiture, and he died after midday and was buried on the right side of Brother Oetbert. He wrote in excellent wise the Chants in the books that are for use in the choir, for he was a good singer, and a man of modest character, and showed himself to be able and skilled in divers kinds of work at harvest time and in the building of the House. When we were driven forth he went with the Brothers to Frisia, though he was weak, for he chose rather to share their exile than to abide alone with a few Lay Brothers to keep the House. But afterward he was sent back before the rest, for his sickness compelled us to do this: so having fulfilled thirty-one years in the Religious Life, he fell asleep in the Lord.

In the year 1431, on the Feast of St. Stephen, Pope and Martyr, Brother Goswin Becker died in Lunenkerc. He was in the beginning of the third year after his profession, but was not yet in Holy Orders, and he was buried in the cloister of the monastery there. He was the son of one John Limborgh, otherwise Becker, and was born at Zwolle.

CHAPTER XXIII.

Of the return of our Brothers from Frisia to Mount St. Agnes.

In the year of our Lord 1422 (1432), license was granted to members of the Religious Orders, and to devout Priests and Canons, to return to their own places and monasteries which they had left in order to observe the Interdict of our Lord the Pope, but some few were excepted as being suspected of taking part in the sedition. Now the Bishop of Matiskon had been sent as Legate of the Apostolic See to make terms of peace, and to remove the Interdict that had been pronounced to maintain the cause of Sueder as against the noble Rodolph, who had been chosen to be Bishop. Many Prelates and Religious Brothers were gathered together to meet the aforesaid Legate in the town of Viana, and the Fathers of our Religious Order and Devotion, the Priors of Windesem and of Mount St. Agnes together with many others—devout Priests, who had been obedient to the Interdict—entered into Utrecht rejoicing, after holding friendly converse with the Legate. Then the Brothers returned each to his own House bearing with them sheaves of peace, the reward for their long exile which they had endured outside the diocese, and so by little and little they returned to their own monasteries eagerly and with devotion; for some of the Brothers of our House returned on the eve of the Feast of the Assumption of the Blessed Mary, and some about the Feast of St. Michael, while a few were left in Frisia to minister to the needs and preserve the discipline of the House at Lunenkerc.

Through all things blessed be God who alone doeth great marvels!

CHAPTER XXIV.

Of the death of Brother John of Kempen, the first Prior of Mount St. Agnes.

In the same year, on the fourth day of November, at midnight, died Brother John of Kempen, the first Rector and Confessor of the Sisters at Arnheim, being in the sixty-seventh year of his age. He had been Rector or Prior in divers places and Houses that were newly founded, namely, at the Fount of the Blessed Virgin, near Arnheim, where he was the first Rector when that House was founded, and here he invested divers Brothers: afterward he was chosen to be Prior of Mount St. Agnes and ruled the House for nine years: then he was sent to Bommel, and he began the House there with a few Brothers. After this he was chosen to be Prior of the House of the Blessed Mary, near Haerlem, in Holland, over which he ruled for seven years. At another time he was deputed to be the first Rector of the Sisters at Bronope, near Kampen, and at last he ended his life happily in a good old age and in obedience in Bethany, which is by interpretation "the House of Obedience," and he was buried within the cloister after Vespers. I was with him and I closed his eyes, for I had been sent by the Visitors to bear him company, and I abode with him for a year and two months. After Easter, in this same year, the House of Bethany was incorporated into the General Chapter.

In the year of the Lord 1433, during Lent, three Clerks were invested, namely, Brother Hermann Craen of Kampen, Brother John Zuermont of Utrecht, and Brother Peter Herbort of Utrecht. In the same year died Sueder of Culenborgh, Bishop of Utrecht, and after his death Pope Eugenius confirmed Rodolph Diepholt, who had been chosen before, to be Bishop of the diocese.

In the year 1434, on the Feast of the Conception of the Glorious Virgin Mary, was invested Brother Bero, a Clerk, of Amsterdam.

In the same year, on July 28th, died Margaret Wilden, a matron of great age and mother of our Brother Oetbert. She was buried in the broad passage at her son's head, and on the northern side of the cloister.

In the year of the Lord 1436, on the Octave of the Feast of St. Stephen, Proto-Martyr, Brother John, the first Convert of our House, died in Beverwijc, near Haerlem. He was a faithful man and prudent in business, wherefore he was sent abroad with Brother Hugo of the same House, and bound by his obedience he accepted the mission.

In the same year, on the Feast of St. Juliana the Virgin, after Lauds, died John Benevolt, a Priest of our House, who was born in Groninghen, a man of great simplicity and innocence; he was buried on the eastern side of the cloister, on the right of Brother John Ummen.

In the same year, on the Feast of the Finding of the Holy Cross, in the first hour after midday, died Brother Alardus, a Priest of Pilsum and a Frisian by nation. He was well stricken in age, being above seventy-six years old, and had lived the Religious Life for thirty years. He was a man of great gentleness, and in the celebration of the Mass careful and devout. He was ever among the first to go into the choir and the Common Refectory of the Brotherhood until his last sickness. It had been his desire to die on this Feast because he had often celebrated it at the Altar of the Holy Cross, and according to his prayer so it was done unto him. He often said to me, "The best dish that is set before me in the Refectory is the Holy Reading, the which I gladly hear: wherefore I do not absent myself willingly lest I should miss the fruit of that Holy Reading during the meal. I delight also in the presence of the Brothers, in that I see the whole congregation there present taking their food under strict discipline." At length he was weighed down with years, and though he could not walk alone, he came leaning upon a staff to the entrance of the choir to hear the Brothers singing; then he took holy water, and bowed the knee toward the High Altar. On the days when he celebrated he often received a special consolation from God Himself.

In the year of the Lord 1438, on the day after the Feast of St. Gregory the Pope, died Brother Rodolph, a Priest from Oetmeshem, who had been Prior of the House of St. Martin the Bishop, in Lunenkerc, in Frisia, near Herlinghen. He had been sick a long while with dropsy, and on the day aforesaid he breathed forth his soul between the ninth and tenth hours in the morning, and he was buried on the right of Brother Alardus. In the same year, on the Feast of the Annunciation of the Blessed Mary ever Virgin, six Clerks were invested, namely, Brother Henry Becker of Zwolle, Brother John Zandwijc of Rhenen, Brother Ewic, also of Rhenen, Brother Telmann Gravensande of Holland, Brother George of Antwerp, and Brother Arnold, son of Conrad, of Nussia. In the same year there was a great famine in divers parts of the land, and in a short space a mighty pestilence followed; also in that year, on the Vigil of the Nativity of Christ, and after High Mass, died John Eme, a Convert, who was cellarer to our House.

In the year of the Lord 1439, on the Feast of St. Peter ad Vincula, and early in the morning, before the fourth hour, died Wermbold Stolwic of Kampen, who was a Priest before he began the Religious Life. He was often sick of a fever, and being weakened thereby he fell asleep in the Lord, having made a good confession, and was buried after Vespers. He wrote the music in some of the Chant books in the choir.

In the same year, on the Feast of the Annunciation of the Virgin Mary, there was an earthquake in divers places, and in the summer following a great pestilence in divers parts, and many devout Brothers and Sisters departed from this present world.

In the year 1440 the great building on the western side of the monastery was set up, to receive guests and the Lay folk of our household, and the roof thereof was finished in stone on the day before the Feast of our Holy Father Augustine. At this work many of our Brothers laboured long and bravely, while others attended to the choir.

In the same year four brothers died in the pestilence, namely, Brother Arnold Droem, a Convert, Goswin Witte, a Clerk and

Oblate, Dirk Mastebroick, a Donate, Hermann Sutor, a Novice. Likewise many of our neighbours in Haerst and Bercmede died of this plague, and by their own desire were buried in our monastery.

In the year of the Lord 1441, on the Feast of St. Petronilla the Virgin, died our beloved Brother Christian of Kampen, the Infirmarius, for he was smitten with the plague. He was very attentive to the sick and plague stricken, to whom he ministered faithfully to the death. On the same day, when noon was hardly past, died John Clotinc, a Lay Brother and Oblate. He was a man very devout, and a pattern for his long service in the brewery and the mill, and for his frequent prayers. These died on the same day and at the same hour after High Mass when Sext was done, and after Vespers, when the Vigils had been sung, they were buried in peace. After their death, by the mercy of God, the plague in the cloister was stayed.

In the same year and month, but before the aforesaid Brothers, and on the day before the Feast of St. Pancras, died the elder Wermbold, a Donate, who was born in Hasselt.

In the year 1442, on the fourth day of March, which was the third Sunday in Lent, the venerable man, John of Korke, Bishop Suffragan to our Lord of Utrecht, consecrated the burial-ground upon the eastern side of the church, together with the cloister thereof, likewise the passage before the Brothers' Refectory, and that on the western side that goeth from before the cells of the Converts to the entrance of the church. Also on the northern side the ground to bury strangers in, with the whole circuit thereof, but the part in the midst of it had been consecrated aforetime with our church. Moreover, the Bishop granted indulgences for forty days to them that walked devoutly round the burial-ground. Besides these, he consecrated the precious and fair Image of the Blessed Virgin with the Child Jesus, that standeth above the altar which is dedicated in honour of Her and of St. Augustine (this is that altar which is set in the midst of the church before the choir), and he granted forty days' indulgence to them that should recite five Aves devoutly and on bended knees before the said image. Likewise, he consecrated another small image of the Blessed Virgin, that is placed before the gate of our monastery, and he granted forty days' indulgence to them that should recite three Aves there devoutly and on bended knees.

In the year of the Lord 1443, on the day of St. Prisca, Virgin and Martyr, and after midday, died our beloved Brother, John Bouman, a Priest, who was once our Procurator. He had been sick for a long while with a quartan fever, whereby his body was wasted, and he finished his life with a happy agony. He was born in Zwolle, and for many years endured labours and divers infirmities, and this saying of Christ was often in his mouth: "In your patience ye shall possess your souls." When I visited him at the end he said to me, "How gladly I would every day go with the Brothers into the choir if I were strong enough God knoweth!" He was full of faith and compassion, and he gladly read and heard of the Passion of our Lord Jesus Christ; he had, moreover, a special devotion to the Blessed Mary Magdalene, for he was born on Her Feast Day, wherefore he often said the Mass for Her Feast, or humbly asked another to say it for him. About a month before his death a certain Brother had this vision after Matins: it seemed to him that the Brothers were singing the Vigil in the choir, and that a corpse was there. And after the Vigil the door of the choir was opened, and certain Lay Brothers of our household came into the choir and stood round the corpse; amongst these were seen two Lay Brothers who were already dead that came to the burial, namely, Brother John Eme and Hermann, son of Wolter (now they had died four years before this time). These, with the rest of the household, went forth as if to follow the corpse going through the gate upon the south side of the choir, and they went in procession to that part of the precinct where our Brothers, who are Priests, are wont to be buried—and straightway the vision disappeared. Then that Brother held his peace and began to think within himself: "It may be that some one of our Brothers shall soon depart out of this world, and we shall sing the solemn Vigils of the dead for him." And so it came to pass, for when the month was ended, Brother John Bouman died, and the things seen in the vision were fulfilled in due order on his behalf, and he was buried near Brother Christian. He lived in the Order of Regulars for thirty-one years and twenty-six days, and he had friends in Zwolle that were good men and great: moreover, notable increase of goods came to our monastery from him and from his parents.

In the year of the Lord 1444, on the Feast of All Saints, was invested Henry Ruhorst, a Clerk, who was born at Kampen.

In the same year, on the Octave of the Assumption of the Blessed Virgin Mary, the Regulars of Haerlem, by the will of all, took upon them the rule of the cloister.

After the Feast of St. Bartholomew, three of our Brothers who were Priests, were sent to found the new House of Roermund.

In the year of the Lord 1445, on the day before the Feast of St. Bernard the Abbot, our beloved Brother Caesarius Coninc died. He was a native of Utrecht, and Prior of Lunenkerc, but he had made his profession at Mount St. Agnes. He went on the concerns of his House to Antwerp, where he fell sick, and having been in a fever for nearly eight days he fell asleep in the Lord, and was buried there in the Convent of the Sisters of our Order. He held the office of Prior for eight years, and he departed from this world in the forty-sixth year of his age, and many goods came for the use of the monastery from his parents.

In the same year, during Advent and after, a flood of waters overwhelmed many lands and drowned the crops in Betua that pertains to Geldria and Hertzogenbusch.

In the year 1446, on the Feast of the Annunciation of the Blessed Virgin Mary, two Clerks were invested, namely, Brother James Spaen, from Geldria, and Brother Henry, son of Paul of Mechlin in Brabant; the former of these attended the school at Deventer, and had a brother who was a Religious at Northorn: the latter attended the school at Zwolle.

In the same year, on Palm Sunday in the month of April, there was a great tempest, snow, hail, and the breath of the storm, and thunder was heard therewith. In the night of that day the dyke between Wilsen and Kampen was broken down, and the cattle and beasts of burden at Mastebroic were drowned. In Zutphen the tower of the church was set afire by lightning, and the roof was cleft above, and certain persons were wounded, and some were slain by this sudden mischance—in other parts also divers houses were destroyed by fire. In Zwolle, after Mass, a mighty terror fell upon them that were in the church, and the shutters were shaken from the church windows by a lightning stroke. In the same year, on the day following the Feast of St. Odulphus, and at the seventh hour when Compline was done, died Brother Frederic, son of John, a Convert from Groninghen. He was an aged man of about eighty years, and one of the elders amongst them that first dwelt in this place. In many things he was profitable to the Brothers, for he shaved their heads and blooded them and dressed their wounds, and did other faithful service to the sick and the plague stricken; at length, wearied with age and having a good foundation of holy deeds, he fell asleep in the Lord. He came to Mount St. Agnes to serve the Lord in the sixth year after the death of Master Gerard Groote, with the first Brothers that dwelt here, and with those very poor Lay folk, the disciples of Gerard, of whom I have written above. He lived therefore in this place for sixty-six years, reckoning the years of his conversion from the beginning thereof to the year of his death inclusively, and Brother John Kempen, the first Prior of this House, invested him as a Convert on the Feast of St. Katharine the Virgin, in the year of the Lord 1401, he being the third of the Converts then invested.

In the same year, on the Octave of the Holy Trinity, and on the night of the Feast of the Saints Gervase and Protasius, died Brother Arnold, son of Conrad of Nussia, being twenty-six years of age. He had been in the priesthood for one year, and for nearly fifteen days had been sick of a tertian fever, but God had pity on him that in a brief space he fulfilled many years, and by the swiftness of his course escaped the hazardous defilements of the world; now he had finished eight years in the Religious Life.

In the year of the Lord 1447, on the day before the Feast of St. Agnes the Virgin, two Clerks were invested, namely, Everard ter Huet of Zwolle and James Spenghe of Utrecht.

In the same year the Clerks at Alberghen, near Oldenzale, received the habit of Holy Religion in the Order of Canons Regular of St. Augustine, and they were invested on the day of the Finding of the Holy Cross.

CHAPTER XXV.

How Theodoric of Kleef, third Prior of the House on the Mount laid down his office, and was absolved therefrom.

In the year of the Lord 1447, that venerable Father, Theodoric of Kleef, third Prior of our House of Mount St. Agnes the Virgin, coming home from the General Chapter, called the Brothers together, and humbly sought to speak with them so that when the Visitors of the House came he might be absolved from his office of Prior. For twenty-three years he had ruled the House with fatherly care, and he was weary with many labours. He would have made this petition a year before, but that the urgency of divers concerns of the House had hindered him from so doing, and he pleaded the weakness of his age and that his senses were clouded. Hearing these things the elder Brothers spake with the members of the Chapter, and thinking to show mercy toward their beloved Father who had long served them to the best of his power, they gave a kindly hearing and assent to his petition. Wherefore the three eldest amongst them, on behalf of the other Brothers and at their request, came to the Visitors, for they were sitting in a private room to hear the opinion of each one of the Brothers, and on bended knees with their hands clasped they besought them instantly, and with all their hearts, to grant absolution to this Father for that he was infirm and aged; this they said was the time to show him pity, and this was what he desired as he had told to certain of them privately.

The Visitors therefore heard the opinions of all, and finding that the more part of them that were gathered together demanded this thing of set purpose, did piously admonish the Prior that he might yield to the petition of the Brothers and resign his office out of consideration for his own weakness of body. The good Father hearing this prostrated himself humbly before the Chapter, and returning thanks to the Brothers said that he was ready to resign into the hands of the Prior of the Superior House the burden of that office which he had long borne.

But since the duty of holding visitations at certain other houses had been laid upon them, the Priors of Windesem and Zwolle besought our Brothers that such visitations might be held by the known and former Prior as the Chapter had ordained, and when these were done, then at a convenient season the desire of the Brothers concerning the absolution of the Prior should be fulfilled.

So when the matter of the visitation was finished, the Priors of Amsterdam and of Hoern returned, and coming to our monastery did a second time examine the opinion of the Brothers in private, and they found that the more part were still of one heart, and constant to their opinion that the Prior should be absolved, though some few of the younger Brothers dissented from the rest.

Hearing this the Visitors, by the authority to them committed, absolved the Prior on the day after the Dispersion of the Apostles, thinking thereby to provide for the peace and usefulness of the House. Then in accordance with the statutes of the Chapter they bade the Brothers to keep fast for three days for the election of a new Prior; then they returned toward Holland to their houses, since their own needs compelled them so to do, but they besought the venerable Prior of Windesem to deign to be present in person at the election when the Brothers should choose their Prior. And this was done, the grace of God providing for us, so that the petition of the brothers, which they had made long since, came to a good issue in the election of a new Prior, for which election they did invoke the Holy Ghost and poured out prayers to God instantly both in public and in private.

CHAPTER XXVI.

How Brother Henry of Deventer was chosen to be the fourth Prior of the House of Mount St. Agnes.

In the year of the Lord 1448, on the 20th day of June (July), when the three days' fast was ended, the Brothers came together to sing the Mass of the Holy Spirit on the day before the Feast of St. Praxedes the Virgin; but the Mass of the Blessed Virgin had been said in private because it was the Sabbath. Then after the end of Mass, and when Sext was done, the Brothers went forth from the choir to the Chapter House to choose a new Prior; and the venerable Prior of Windesem, with the Prior of Zwolle, was there present with them, for he had been called and besought to hear the election. So, having held a short conference with the Brothers, and the manner of election being read, the Prior of Windesem exhorted the members of the Chapter to choose a fit person to be Prior following the commandments of God and Canon Law. There were here present twenty-one Brothers that were electors, and two who were far away had written letters wherein they expressed their will. So the Brothers that were electors went away a little space outside the doors of the Chapter House, and the two Priors aforesaid came and stood by the altar in the Chapter House, the door thereof being open, and with them were the three elder Brothers. There they stood to hear the votes of each man separately, for they could be seen by all, but none could hear what was said. Then the votes of each being heard and counted, our Sub-Prior, Brother Henry, son of William of Deventer, was chosen and nominated to be Prior, having the votes of the more part recorded for him on the paper, namely sixteen. Some there were beside that did not choose him, but of these three Brothers did not vote at this time, and two chose the Procurator, James Cluyt. Then one of the elder Brothers, on behalf of himself and of the more part, besought the Prior of the Superior House to confirm the election, who straightway appointed the next day to be the last for any to oppose. And when none made opposition to the manner of the election, nor said aught against the Brother who was chosen, the Prior elect was called to consent to his election which had been made according to the canons, so that it might be duly confirmed. And he straightway prostrated himself in the midst of the Brothers protesting that he was not sufficient, and he humbly besought to be relieved of this burden, but when he could not gain his purpose, and dared not obstinately to resist, he gave consent in an humble voice, being overcome by the insistence of the Brothers and compelled by his obedience to his superior: and he submitted himself to the ordinance of God for the sake of observing brotherly love and the needful discipline of the cloister. So when he had been confirmed by the Prior of Windesem he was led in to the choir in the presence of all the Brothers, and placed in his stall, and prayers were offered up. After which done all the members of the Chapter straightway went into the House, and following the accustomed manner all the professed Brothers took the vow of obedience to their Father, the new Prior, and after them the Converts, and lastly the Donates did the like. When this was done they spent the day with joy and giving of thanks, and at last their Fathers, the Priors of the other houses who had taken part in all that was done, said farewell to them, and the Brothers left the garden and returned to their cells. When the bell rang for Vespers they came together to the choir, and sang the Vespers of St. Mary Magdalene with cheerful voices. After three days the Brothers were called together to the Chapter House, and the Prior proposed that in accordance with the statutes they should choose another Sub-Prior, so on the Feast of St. James the Apostle, before the hour for Vespers, Brother Thomas of Kempen was nominated and elected after a brief scrutiny. He was one of the elders, being sixty-seven years of age, and in past times had been appointed to this office, and albeit he knew himself to be insufficient and would have made excuse, yet he did submit him humbly to the assembled Brothers, for his obedience bade him so to do; neither did he refuse to undergo toil on their behalf for the love of Christ Jesus, but earnestly besought the prayers of his comrades and Brothers, for he trusted rather in the grace of God than in himself.

In the same year, during the summer season, the crops were grievously ravaged in divers places by the mice, which ate the corn while it was still growing up and when it was in the blade. Our Lay Brothers, therefore, dug ditches and put in the ground jars filled with water, and such was the craft with which they did this that a vast number of the mice were drowned in these jars, and they slew in divers places many thousands. These creatures had caused great loss to us and our neighbours by ravaging the wheat, the barley, the oats, and the peas, and also the green crops in the fields that were for the fodder of the cattle.

About the beginning of the month of September there was a notable tempest, and a great flood of waters broke in upon us (for the sea had burst his banks), and this did overflow our pasture land and destroyed the grass and the fodder. By this same tempest many ships that had adventured themselves upon the sea were overwhelmed with all their crews.

But herein again the good and merciful God did provide for us, for our fishers took great store of fish by reason of this flood, and these did suffice the Brothers and their guests for food during many days.

In the year of the Lord 1449, on the Feast of St. Bernard the Abbot, we received the precious relics of certain Saints and Martyrs who were companions of Gereon, Duke and Martyr, and of others that were companions of the Eleven Thousand Holy Virgins of Cologne. These did the venerable Abbot of St. Panthalion send to us from the many relics that are in that monastery.

Likewise Egbert Tyveren, a Donate of our House, brought back to us from Cologne, as true relics, certain small fragments that were given to us by the Carthusians, and by the Regular Brothers of our own order in the House of Corpus Domini. The Prior and the Brothers of our House being gathered together in the choir before High Mass brought these relics into the church, carrying the Standard of the Cross and lighted tapers in their hands, and afterward the Prior placed them on the different altars, having enclosed them in reliquaries in seemly wise in honour of the Saints.

In the same year, on December the 16th, our Brother Godefried of Kempen died in Brabant in the House of the Sisters of the Regular Order that is called the Cloister of the Blessed Virgin, near Zevenborren. This convent was afterward destroyed utterly by fire in the year 14--, and the Sisters were removed to Brussels with great honour by the Duchess of Burgundy.

In the year of the Lord 1450 many faithful servants of Christ went to Rome to gain Indulgences, which our Lord, Pope Nicholas V, by advice of the Cardinals, and moved himself by piety and mercy, had granted by a Bull in the previous year. Then did many Christian folk that sojourned on this holy pilgrimage return whole, but many died by the way, and many in the city of Rome.

In the same year, in Holland, Utrecht, Amersfoort, Zwolle, Kampen, Deventer, Zutphen and many other towns and hamlets, a bubonic plague raged, and many devout persons and religious, as also many worldlings, departed from this present life. In the same year the winter time was very mild, with but little snow and thin ice, but the wind was cold. In Lent, and at the beginning of March, our fishers took great abundance of the fish called smelts, wherewith, during the Fast, our Brothers were fed, and also many poor beggars at our gates.

In the same year the men of Zwolle built a great and lofty bridge of strong wooden timbers across the River Vecht, not far from our monastery, to serve the necessities of their own folk and the convenience of men that would come thither; the cost thereof was six hundred Rhenish florins.

In the same year, on the Feast of St. John before the Latin Gate, Brother Gerard of Deventer, whose surname was Bredenort, was invested.

In the same year, on the twenty-ninth day of August, died James Oem, Rector of the Sisters at Bronope, near Kampen, who for nine years had exercised a kindly rule over that House. After his death the Prior of Windesem appointed Brother Dirk of Kleef to be Rector and Confessor of this House. He had been formerly Prior of Mount St. Agnes, and was the eldest of the Brothers of that monastery.

In the year 1451, on the Octave of Easter, which was the day before the Feast of the Finding of the Holy Cross, died Dirk Poderen, a servant of our House, a poor man and an aged, being about eighty years old: he had lived with us for twenty years.

In the same year, on the Vigil of the Feast of St. Andrew the Apostle, and at the ninth hour, when Compline had been said, died Brother Gerard, son of Wolter, a Convert who was sixty-eight years of age lacking two months, and had lived the Religious Life for nearly forty years. The Prior and the Brothers were present with him at his death: he was faithful and earnest in good deeds and words, and he was buried on the western side of the passage with the other Converts.

In the same year a new mill was builded, and finished with much labour and cost, for the greater convenience of our House.

In the same year the House of the Regulars in Cologne which is called "Corpus Christi," and standeth in the parish of St. Christopher the Martyr, was received into our Chapter. At this time, namely, after the Feast of the Conception of the Blessed Virgin, our Brother, Henry Cremer, was sent to act as Sub-Prior of this House, and Brother Gerard of Kleef went with him to be the Rector.

In the same year there was a grievous pestilence in Cologne, and as is reported by many, twenty-five thousand persons are reckoned to have died thereof.

In the year of the Lord 1451, our most Reverend Lord Nicholas de Chusa, Cardinal with the title of St. Peter in Chains, who was Legate for the land of Germany, came to the diocese of Utrecht, after that he had visited the upper parts of Saxony and the cities and townships of Westphalia. He came likewise to Windesem, where he was received with honour by the Brothers, and held a conference with them, and by the authority of the Apostolic See he granted Indulgences on the occasion of the

Jubilee to all that were subject to our General Chapter. When he was asked whether one might go to Rome to gain Indulgences without special license, he replied: "Our Lord the Pope himself hath said, 'Better is obedience than Indulgences.'"

In the year of the Lord 1452, a great and grievous loss befel the city of Amsterdam, a famed and populous city in Holland, for a fire broke forth on the Feast Day of Urban, Pope and Martyr, and the wrath of God went forth in particular against the congregations of religious persons, both men and women; so great was the fire that the more part of the city should seem to have been destroyed, and scarce a third part thereof was saved. Fourteen monasteries are known to have burned almost to the ground, and verily great misery was caused thereby in the sight of all men, such as had not been heard of from very ancient times until that day. Many virgins that had taken the veil, putting aside their maiden modesty, wandered about the city lamenting and begging for hospitality, whereby the hearts of many were moved to tears. Everything was buried, from the great Church of St. Nicholas to the ancient Convent of the Nuns of our Order inclusively, and in the other direction from the Church of the Blessed Virgin Mary to our monastery exclusively, for God in His mercy spared that House that it was unhurt.

In the same year, on the Feast of the Commemoration of St. Paul the Apostle, and after Vespers, our beloved Brother Henry Cremer died at Windesem; on the day following, being the Octave of St. John the Baptist, his body was brought to our House, wherein, through the mercy of God, he had lived for nearly thirty-three years in the Religious habit; this was done that at his life's end he might not lie in a strange land afar from our House, but might be buried according as he desired amongst our Brothers. He was faithful in his labour, in the writing of books, and in his attendance in the choir; and being zealous for discipline he kept a watch over his mouth and loved his cell. Formerly he had been Prior in Rickenberrich in Saxony for nearly eleven years, and afterward for a few years abode in Diepenveen with two others his companions, but he was instant in his petition to return to the Brotherhood, and obtained his desire; after this he was sent to Cologne, but returning thence he died at Windesem and was buried in our House.

In the year of the Lord 1453, a strange pestilence fell upon the men of certain towns and the villages adjacent thereto. This plague befel after the Feast of St. John the Baptist, and was notable by reason of the benumbing of the throat and the pain it caused in the breast and side. At this time many of our Brothers and the Lay folk of our Household who were labouring hard in the fields—for it was harvest—were smitten so grievously by the benumbing of their throats that they could scarce speak or eat. There was a north wind that was very cold at night, but by day turbulent and dry, and many were chilled thereby and fell sick. As a remedy against this, some clothed themselves in stouter garments and abstained from cold food and drink, and these grew well by reason of their abstinence and care to keep themselves from too great cold, for God had pity on them; but some that neglected these matters died after three days, or even two, being weakened by the numbness.

When this disease first broke forth, our Brother Gerard ter Mollen, a Convert, fell sick and received the Unction after Compline on the day of the Translation of St. Martin the Bishop: in the night following, before the hour for Matins, his sickness grew heavy on him and he died. He was a faithful labourer, ever ready to toil for the common weal, and he was in the sixtieth year of his age, having fulfilled thirty years and three months in the Religious Life: he was buried in the western path at the head of Gerard, son of Wolter.

In the same year, in the month of July, and on the Feast of the Translation of Benedict the Abbot, died Dirk, son of Arnold, a young man who was a Laic and Fellow Commoner, that came from Bericmede: he had received the Sacrament of the Holy Unction, and died after High Mass had begun.

In the same month, on the day following the Feast of St. Margaret the Virgin, when Compline was done, and the Ave Maria had been said, died Henry Diest, a Donate of our House:

he was nearly forty-eight years of age and had fulfilled thirty years in this House.

In the same month, on the day following the Feast of Alexius the Confessor, Dirk Struve, a Laic and Fellow Commoner, died after Compline, having received the Holy Rite of Extreme Unction. He had lived long in the House, and on the day following when the first Mass had been said he was laid in the burying ground of the Lay Brothers.

After him, and on the night before the Feast of St. Mary Magdalene, before Matins, died Everard Ens of Campen, a good and faithful Laic and Fellow Commoner, who had lived with us for fifteen years.

In the same year, in the month of August, on the night before the Feast of St. Dominic the Confessor, and before Matins, died our most beloved Brother Theodoric of Kleef. He was the third Prior of our House, and an old man and full of days, for he was seventy-six years old, and had fulfilled fifty-five years in the Religious Life. When the first Brothers were invested here, he was the fourth to receive the Habit, and from the very beginning of the monastery, before any of the Brothers had received investiture, he with the Clerks and Lay folk in this place had begun to serve the Lord in much poverty and toil. Moreover, it had always been his desire that by the favour of the Lord he might end his life in this same House with the Brothers, and be buried amongst them, and so it came about, for he was laid in the eastern passage by the side of our Brother, Henry Cremer, whom he had drawn to the Religious Life, and whom he had loved with all his heart. Thus it came about that as they had loved one another in life, so in death and in the grave they were not divided.

In the same year and month, on the day following the Feast of Sixtus, Pope and Martyr, and when noon was past, died Dirk, son of Wychmann of Arnheim, who had lived here for two years.

In the same year, in the month of August, on the Feast of St. Lawrence the Martyr, and in the morning after Prime, died Matthias, son of William of Overcamp, a Donate of our House, who had been overseer of husbandry for a great while. He often suffered pain from the stone, and at length falling sick with a disease in the throat, and being bowed with age, he fell on sleep in holy peace in the seventy-second year of his age, having endured many labours; for when the monastery was founded he came hither with his father, William, a tailor, of great age, and being then but ten years old, he began that good course which was brought to this happy issue. He was laid in the burying-ground of the Lay folk before the entrance to the broad cloister. At this time of pestilence in our House it befel that a certain Brother, while sitting in his cell, heard a sound at the door thereof as of one knocking twice, but when he arose to open the door he could not see or find any man there. And marvelling at the matter he thought that perhaps some one might be like to die, and on the next day the bell was tolled for the death of Dirk Struve, a Laic of our household. So also before the death of Brother Theodoric of Kleef, once the Prior of our House, the like thing happened two days before he fell sick.

In the year 1454, on the morning of the fourteenth day of March and after Prime, died Brother Gerard Hombolt, a Convert, in the fifty-fifth year of his age. He had fulfilled thirty years in the Religious Life, and for a great while was cellarer of the House, in which office he was faithful and zealous for the common good, so far as our poverty in temporal wealth and the number of persons to be served did allow. He was buried in the western passage before the door of the church with the other Converts.

In the same year, on the sixteenth day of May, the venerable Father John Lap died in the House of Elisabethdal, near Roremund, of which he was Prior, but he had made his profession as a Brother of our House of Mount St. Agnes. He was in the fifty-fifth year of his age, and being a lover of discipline and of the Religious Life had fulfilled thirty years and nearly two months therein.

In the same year, on the day before the Feast of the Exaltation of the Holy Cross, and about the second hour after noon, died Dionysius Valkenborch, a Donate of our House, being seventy-three years of age. He had lived an humble and holy life with us for a great while, near to fifty-five years; at first his tasks were to feed the swine and milk the cows, but when he grew old he was made the gatekeeper, with another to help him, and ending his temporal life in a good old age he left a fair ensample to all.

In the same year, in the month of August, on the day following the Feast of the Assumption of the Blessed Virgin Mary, there was a heavy rain both in the uplands and the lowlands, and much corn and seed perished thereby, and we suffered great loss in our farm by the overflowing of many waters. In the same year, on the Feast of Gallus the Confessor, and at about the ninth hour, when Compline was ended, died Brother John Zandwijc of Renen, a Priest of our House, being thirty-eight years old. He had suffered long from the stone, and was patient and gentle, and he had fulfilled sixteen years and near seven months in the Religious Life. On the day before the Feast of St. Luke, when Mass was ended, he was buried by the side of Theodoric of Kleef in the eastern passage of the cloister; here he rests in peace, freed from the many toils and perils of this life, for his desire was to be released and to be with Christ.

In the year 1455, on the Feast of the Conversion of St. Paul, two Clerks were invested, namely, Brother Henry, son of Bruno, and Theodoric, son of Arnold Wanninck; both came from Deventer, and had honourable parents and friends, and in the year following they made their profession together upon the same day.

In the same year, on the Octave of the Feast of the Apostles Peter and Paul, when Matins was ended, died our venerable Father, William Voerniken, the fourth Prior of Windesem. He was buried in the choir by the side of the venerable Prior John Huesden, for these two greatly loved one another, wherefore after death they shared one tomb in the church. He was eighty-two years of age, and had been the second Prior of the House on Mount St. Agnes.

In the same year, on the 22nd of April, when Prime was done, died John Mastebroick, a Laic and servant of our House, who was faithful in labour and devout in prayer. He was about seventy years old, and had lived with us for nearly forty-five years, and he departed to the Lord in holy peace, desiring an eternal reward for his many labours. He was laid with the servants in the burial-ground of the Lay folk and Donates of our House.

In the same year, on the 9th of October, the day before the Feast of Marcus, Pope and Confessor, when Compline was done, died Gerard, son of Hermann, a Laic and servant of our House; he was a stonemason and a faithful worker so far as his powers did allow, but he was often sick with the complaint of the stone, from the tortures whereof he died, though he bore the same with much patience; and he left all the goods he had as a bequest to the monastery.

In the year of the Lord 1455, on the 17th day of November, within the Octave of the Feast of St. Martin the Bishop, four altars in our church were consecrated by Iodocus, who was Bishop Suffragan, Doctor in Sacred Theology, and belonged to the order of Preachers. He had received a general commission from the General Chapter of Utrecht, and he consecrated the several altars after this wise. First the altar which is on the north of the church, and in the upper part thereof, in honour of St. Michael the Archangel and all the holy Angels: secondly, the altar which standeth upon the same side, but in the lower part of the church, in honour of the holy Confessors, Gregory, Ambrose, Jerome, Bernard, Francis, and Lebuin. Thirdly, the altar which is in the midst of the church, in honour of the holy Confessors, Martin the Bishop, Willibrord the Bishop, Nicholas the Bishop, and Antony the Confessor. Fourthly, the altar which standeth on the south side, toward the end of the church, in honour of the Saints Anne, Elizabeth, Monica, mother of our holy Father Augustine, and all holy widows.

Likewise he consecrated the Holy Cross that is over the door of the choir, and certain images of Saints, namely, of St. Augustine the Bishop and St. Agnes the Virgin: also two small figures, the first of St. Mary Magdalene, the second of St. Agnes in the Coffer; also the image that is over the altar of the Holy

Cross that showeth the blessed Virgin Mary holding the Crucified Lord, Who lieth on her breast: also the images of St. James the Apostle, St. Katherine the Virgin, and St. Barbara, Virgin and Martyr.

In the year of the Lord 1456, on the Feast of St. Antony the Confessor, Brother Gerard, son of Dirk, who came from a place near Zwolle, was invested as a Convert. He was a man well stricken in age, and had lived with us in honest wise for thirty years, being a good husbandman; before his investiture he had been an humble Donate, for we had many of that degree amongst us.

In the same year, on the day following the Feast of St. James the Apostle, died John Smyt, a Laic and servant of our House. He was drowned in a deep pool that had been filled by the rain, and with him perished four very good horses that were drawing a cart to fetch fodder. At that time the weather was very rainy, so that many crops were destroyed thereby. The Brothers therefore brought back this servant of God to the House, and after Compline laid him in the burial-ground of the Laics. Moreover, they celebrated Mass for him, and offered up prayers that he might receive the reward of his labours. By God's providence, he and the other Laics of our House had received Communion, as was the custom, on St. James's day: and he himself had lived with us for one year, being skilful and diligent in the smith's craft.

In all things blessed be God, Who scourgeth us, and also healeth our stripes, for though we lost above an hundred florins by the drowning of the horses, yet did the good Lord save us and our country from the army of the Duke of Burgundy, who was laying siege to Deventer; for after the Feast of St. Matthew peace and concord were restored between the Duke and the cities and people of this land.

In the same year of the Lord 1456, on the Feast day of St. Lucia, Virgin and Martyr, and in the morning when High Mass for her festival was already begun, died that fervent lover of discipline, Brother William Coman. He was born in Amsterdam, in Holland, and for a great while had lived an humble life amongst our Brothers, and he was seventy-eight years and four months old. On the Feast of St. Brixius, Bishop and Confessor, he had fulfilled, by the help of God, fifty-five years in the Religious Life, for this was the anniversary of his investiture, and on this day he celebrated Mass for the last time, for he was sick from that day forward until the Feast day of St. Lucia, whereon he ended his life with a happy agony; and he was buried in the eastern passage by the side of our Brother John Zantwijc.

This William Coman left many a good ensample of patience, poverty, and abstinence, for the imitation of them that come after; and in the days of the venerable Prior, William Vorniken (who was the second to hold that office in our House) he was Procurator, and afterwards Sub-Prior. Then for three years he was Prior of the House at Amersfoort, after which he was Rector of the Sisters at Bronope near Kampen for fourteen years; but at last, as age had come upon him, and his hearing failed by little and little, he returned to our House and Brotherhood, where he died in holy peace, and he was buried amongst the Brothers after the accustomed manner.

In the same year died Gerard Smullinc, the first Rector and Prior of the House at Ruremund, who, after that he was absolved from his office, went to gain Indulgences at the Shrine of St. James at Compostella, in which place he was buried.

The anniversary of his death and that of his parents is kept on the day following the Feast of St. Elizabeth, because we know not surely the day thereof.

In the year of the Lord 1457, on the day of St. Benedict the Abbot, and at eleven o'clock at night, Theodoric Herxen, a venerable Father of pious memory, and a priest of seemly life, died at Zwolle, being seventy-six years old. He was the second Rector of the House of Clerks in Zwolle, and ruled it for forty-seven years; also he was Confessor to many devout Brothers and Sisters, and his whole life, from the time that he was of full age, was spent in discipline of character and in virtue.

CHAPTER XXVII.

How Father Henry, the fourth Prior, resigned his office, and how Father George was chosen to be the fifth Prior.

In the year 1458, on the day following the Feast of St. Matthias the Apostle, Brother Henry, son of William, the fourth Prior of the House, resigned his office. Now he had lain sick for a great while and was weak from fever; wherefore, prostrate upon his bed in the presence of all the Brothers, he besought them with many tears and exhorted them to agree to choose another Prior in his room, according to the lawful statutes of the Order.

Hearing this all the Brothers were grieved, and for three days they fasted after the accustomed manner, praying for guidance in the coming election, which was held on the Thursday after the third Sunday in Lent, for which day the Introit is "Mine eyes are ever toward the Lord." So when the Mass of the Holy Spirit had been said and the hours were done, the election was held in the choir in the presence of all the Brothers; and that venerable Father the Prior of Windesem was also present with them to hear the opinion of each one; likewise Brother John Naeldwijc and Brother James of Cologne, Prior of the House of the Blessed Virgin at Belheem in Zwolle.

When the opinion of each had been heard, George, who was a Brother of our House, but at this time Prior of Briel, was chosen by the greater number of votes. Some indeed chose Bero, Prior of Beverwijc, but all consented humbly and peaceably to the judgment of the greater number; so by common consent Brother George was elected, being a Father most beloved, and himself a lover of the rule.

In the same year four Brothers were invested, three of them on the day following the Feast of St. George the Martyr, and the names of these were Henry Hierde of Herderwijc in Geldria, Hermann Borken of Westphalia in the diocese of Munster, and Theodoric of Zwolle. The fourth, namely, John Orsoy of Kleef, was invested soon after, on the Feast of the birthday of our Father St. Augustine.

In the same year there was a notable pestilence in Deventer, Zwolle, and Kampen, the which had raged in Utrecht and the neighbouring places in the previous year. Verily this scourge of God was pious and pitiful towards Christian folk, as hindering them from dwelling long in this world so as to love it rather than the kingdom of Heaven. At this time many devout Sisters in Deventer and Zwolle departed to Christ.

On the day following the Feast of the Nativity of the Blessed and Glorious Virgin Mary died our beloved Brother Henry Ruhorst, the Sub-Prior of our House, being forty years old, and he was buried in the eastern cloister by the side of our Brother William Coman.

In the same year and month, on the Feast of St. Jerome and after midday, died Hermann, son of John, a Laic who was Sub-Infirmarius, being twenty-six years old. He was a poor man, who was born in a place near Wessel in the district of Kleef; and being received by us, he showed himself ready to do whatever was laid upon him.

In the same year, in the month of October, and at noon on the Feast day of St. Dionysius the Bishop, Brother Gerard Wessep died in Zwolle. He had been sent to the Monastery of Belheem, and of his obedience and brotherly love he went thither after the death of many of the Brothers of the House; for of these ten had died, as well as certain Laics that were of the household. After the hour of Vespers he was borne to a carriage and brought therein to our House, as he had desired, and he was buried with the Brothers in the eastern cloister, by the side of the Sub-Prior. At the time of his death he had fulfilled almost fifty-six years in the Order, being in the seventy-seventh year of his age. He wrote many books in the Latin and Teutonic tongues for the choir, the library, and for sale; and he was forward to perform many labours for the common good. Above all he was very faithful and ready in tending the sick and dying till the moment of their departure; for he feared not then to tend and stand by diseased and plague stricken folk, serving them for the sake of God and brotherly love. So the Lord willed to reward him also, with the Brothers that were dead in Belheem; wherefore, when he had spent fifteen days in Zwolle, he fell sick of the plague, and God took him from the toil and trouble of this present life and gave him eternal peace and rest, which things—as oft he told me with clasped hands—he had long desired.

In the same year, on the day following the Feast of St. Martin the Bishop, at the hour of Vespers, died our beloved Brother James Cluit, a devout Priest and first Rector of Udem, being sixty-three years old, and he was buried before the High Altar. His memory shall continue to be praised and blessed, for he was beloved of God, an ensample to us all, and his own stern judge.

In the year of the Lord 1459, on the Feast of the Epiphany and at about the fifth hour in the morning before Prime, died Everard of Wetteren, the cook, a devout Donate, who was eighty years of age and over. He had dwelt formerly in Deventer with Lambert Gale, a tailor, and in the days of Florentius, who sent him to Windesem, he was first tailor of the House; but the Brothers at Windesem sent him on to Mount St. Agnes before the members of that community were invested with the Religious habit, and there he helped to sew and make the garments in which those first four Brothers were habited, whose investiture in the year 1398 is described above. After some while spent in this office he was sent to serve in the kitchen as assistant, and he afterwards became chief cook, in which post he served all the Brothers faithfully for above thirty years. At length, wearied with years, he was relieved from his labours and slept in peace, being an old man and full of many days.

In the same year, within the Octave of the Nativity of the Blessed Virgin Mary and on the Feast day of the holy martyrs Protus and Hyacinthus, at noon died Gerard Hombolt of Utrecht, a Donate of our House, who was fifty-nine years old. He was very zealous, faithful, and devout in the service of God, particularly in the things which pertain to the glory and honour of the Blessed Virgin Mary; moreover, he procured a most fair image of her, and a corona of polished brass holding many candles, and certain other ornaments that are set above the altar of the Blessed Virgin. These things he did out of his great devotion, and with a pious intention of adorning our church in honour of the Blessed Virgin and St. Agnes.

First he was Hospitarius and afterward Refectorarius to the Brothers, and all things that were committed to his charge he kept honestly and in cleanly fashion, seeing to the provision of all needful vessels, napkins, and towels. On a time when many guests had come to the House he bade the cook provide all things necessary for them; but the cook, being troubled at this unaccustomed number, was heavy at heart, for he feared lest he might not be able to satisfy all as he fain would do, but Gerard Hombolt, putting his trust in the Lord, said, "Make the sign of the Holy Cross over the pots and the cooked food and God shall give His blessing and a sufficiency." So the cook did as Gerard had said, and blessed the provision again and again in faith, and behold the good Lord, seeing their faith, gave them an increase so that all had enough; and when the meal was done there was abundance left over, insomuch that the fragments that remained sufficed for a full meal at supper.

In his youth, and before he entered the monastery, Gerard, out of his great devotion, visited the Holy Land—Jerusalem, Bethlehem, and the other places hallowed by our Saviour; and he was disposed, if it should be allowed him, to visit them once again before his death. But the good Lord changed his love for the earthly Jerusalem to love for the Jerusalem which is in Heaven, into which he entered (as I hope) through the intercession of the Blessed and Glorious Virgin; for on all the Vigils before Her feasts it was his wont to fast, eating nought save bread nor drinking aught save beer; and it was within the Octave of the Feast of Her Nativity that he departed in holy peace out of this present world to the realms of Heaven, having made a good confession, being contrite, and having received the Unction. Much wealth also came to our House through his means, and he died in the fifty-ninth year of his age, having lived with us for thirty-five years.

In the year of the Lord 1460, after the Feast of the Purification of the Blessed Virgin Mary, there was a mighty frost. The bitter cold began on the Feast day of St. Scholastica the Virgin (which was the first Sunday in Lent), and endured until the middle of the fast, so that men and horses heavily laden could walk everywhere upon the frozen waters in safety, and carry their goods across the same. Likewise in many places there was lack of fodder and straw wherewith to feed the beasts, for the ground was dry and frost bound, wherefore men could not get them fresh grass to feed the cattle. For this cause some poor men brake up the roofs of their houses and gave of the thatch to the beasts: and this lack of grass endured until the first of May.

In the same year, in the month of April, and on the second Sunday after Easter, which was the day before the Feast of Vitalis the Martyr, Brother Gerard Cortbeen was invested: he was a Priest, and a native of Herderwijc, a good man, honest, faithful, and thirty-two years of age.

In the same year our church was adorned in seemly wise, the roof thereof and all the flat spaces of the inner walls being painted in fair colours to the glory of God and in honour of St. Agnes the Patron Saint of the church. Amid the bright colours were written these three names Jesus, Mary, Agnes, which of holy purpose were painted in large and black letters, and they stand forth clearly to be read by the eyes of all that enter the church.

In the same year, on the Feast of the Dispersion of the Apostles, between the hours of Tierce and High Mass, died Deric, son of William, a carpenter and servant of our household who was a Fellow Commoner. He was born in Zwolle and was now thirty years of age, having lived a good, humble, and peaceable life in this House for nearly eleven years.

In the year of the Lord 1461, on the morning of the Feast of St. Emerentiana the Virgin, and before the hour of Prime, died Herder Stael, a very honest man, and a fellow citizen with us at Zwolle, being seventy-four years old. He was a special and faithful friend to our House for many years. As was his wife also particularly in the troubled times of Bishop Rudolph, when our Brothers were constrained to leave the monastery and to go to the House belonging to our Order in Lunenkerc. At that time this good man bought our crops as they stood in the fields near the monastery, and out of an honest purpose bade his servants to reap and harvest the same. Afterward he sent the fruits of the ground, and the provender that had been gathered, to our Brothers in Lunenkerc by little and little, for they had been sent thither as it were to a place of exile. This same Herder Stael lived with us for nearly a year before his death, being moved so to do by a deep desire, and having a holy and firm purpose to serve God. He died as aforesaid in holy peace and in an honoured old age, and his body was laid in the broad cloister; his friends from Zwolle being present at his burial.

CHAPTER XXVIII.

Of the ancient Reliquary of St. Agnes, and how it was gotten.

In the same year 1461, George, the venerable Father of our House, asked and obtained from the Canons of the great church at Utrecht the ancient Reliquary of the most holy Agnes, Virgin and Martyr, and the beloved Patron of our House, but her relics were not therein contained. It was in her honour that our church was consecrated in the year of the Lord 1412, and on the Friday in Easter week, as is set forth more fully above in the chapter entitled "Of the Consecration of our Church."

Two of our Brothers that were ordained to be Priests, namely, Brother Henry, son of Bruno, and Brother Theodoric Wanninck, brought back this holy Reliquary with them, journeying from Utrecht by way of Holland, and across the sea, not without danger and fear, for the sea was turbulent. Yet through the help of God, and the merits of St. Agnes the Virgin, they were protected from these perils and reached an haven of safety. A few days afterward, on the eve of the Feast of St. Scholastica the Virgin, they brought the Reliquary to Mount St. Agnes, and our Brothers, with all the Laics of our household, hearing this, did rejoice exceedingly.

The Reliquary was borne into the church with all devotion and reverence and placed in the sanctuary of the choir near the High Altar and beneath the arch in the northern wall. The bones of the Saint had rested for nearly three hundred and fifty years in this Reliquary, which was an humble one, being of wood and covered with plates of brass and gilded work. But at last a new and most fair coffer of silver adorned with gold was made for her by the Canons of the great Church of St. Martin at Utrecht.

Likewise one should note that it was in the year of the Lord 1413, in the time of Frederick of Blanckenhem, the Reverend Bishop of Utrecht, that the relics of this most Blessed Saint Agnes the Virgin were removed with all reverence from the ancient wooden Reliquary into this new one of silver fairly gilt. This was done on the second of December, being the day following the Feast of Ægidius the Abbot, by that Reverend man Hermann Lochorst, Dean of the great Church of St. Martin the Bishop. He it was, chiefly, who had procured that the holy relics of the Saint should be removed in this manner; and a great while afterward George, our venerable Father and Prior, earnestly begged for the ancient Reliquary, which our House had long desired, and by the insistence of his friends he obtained the same from the Chapter and Canons of the church. These things were done in the year 1461, as is written above.

In the year of the Lord 1462, on the night of the Feast of St. Juliana, Virgin and Martyr, died our beloved Brother John, son of Hessel of Zuermont, who came from Utrecht. He was a timid man, and ready for any lowly task; moreover, his will was always good to serve the monastery to the best of his power. Yet through the weakness of his nature and pains in his head, he often stayed outside the choir, but by his work without he redeemed the time which he could not spend in devotion within the church.

A few days before his death he said to certain of the Brothers that he should die shortly, and indeed the end came somewhat suddenly to him, for on the day before the Feast of Juliana the Virgin he was well and cheerful, but in the night following some weakness, whereof we knew not, came upon him, and he was found dead before the bed in his cell; being clad in his under garment he lay prostrate upon the floor with his feet stretched out and his arms close to his side, looking as though he were commending himself to God and to the Holy Angels: for no man was with him at the last to give him comfort, since none knew of his agony, but after supper-time, because they saw that he was not present, certain Brothers sought him in the cell where he slept, and they found that he was gone away from this world, and had fled to Christ as we do piously hope and believe. He came of very good and honest parents in Utrecht, and had many friends and kinsmen that were living the Religious Life. And so at length, after many labours and much pain of heart and body, he was taken away from the miseries of this present life, in the fifty-fourth year of his age, having spent twenty-nine years in the Religious Life. After the office of the Mass had been said duly, and the Psalms and Vigils had been recited, he was buried in the eastern side of the cloister, on the right of Brother Gerard Wesep.

In the same year, after the Epiphany, there was a most bitter frost, which lasted throughout Lent and longer, and the great drought was hurtful to the pasture lands whereon the beasts were fed.

CHAPTER XXIX.

Of the death of Brother Henry, son of William, the fourth Prior of our House.

In the same year, and upon the 10th day of March, being the second day before the Feast of St. Gregory the Pope, died our most beloved Brother of pious memory, Henry, son of William, who was a native of Deventer. He departed at the fifth hour after midday, when the Vigils of the dead had been sung; and our beloved Father George and all the Brothers were present with him, praying during his happy death struggle, and many Laics of our household were there also.

He had been the fourth Prior of our House, and having sought instantly to be absolved from his office because of his oft infirmities, he lived thereafter for four years amongst the Brothers, being humble, gentle, exemplary, devout, and reverent to all. To none was he burdensome, but to all men kindly, comfortable, pitiful, helpful, cheerful, modest, peaceable, and silent. Amid elders and prelates he was lowly and courteous, towards the young and weakly he was sweet and amiable. Because of his good and modest manners, his uprightness, fidelity, and the honest bearing which he showed (as a Religious ought to do) whether walking or standing, speaking or keeping silence, he long held the office of Procurator for the House; for he was chosen for that post in the first place, and afterward was made Sub-Prior. But at last, by God's ordinance, he was promoted to be the fourth Prior of our community, in which office he was confirmed in all peace and charity. For ten years he continued to be Prior, ruling those that were under him by the goodness and modesty of his character rather than by rough speech; he was instant in his zeal for reading, for prayer, and holy meditations whensoever such exercises were possible. Well might one write and say of him many of those things that the blessed Bernard doth write concerning Humbert, the servant of God, who was the devout Sub-Prior in St. Bernard's House. Him did Henry strive to imitate, for he too was devout, beloved of God and man, and a servant of Christ. He died in the sixty-first year of his age, having entered upon the forty-second year of his Religious Life, and he was buried on the right side of Brother John Zuermont.

In the same year, on the day before the Feast of St. Ambrose the Bishop—this day being the Saturday before Passion Sunday—and at the fifth hour of the morning before Prime, died Dirk ten Water, an honourable citizen and magistrate of Zwolle, who had been received as a Fellow Commoner, for he greatly favoured the devout.

He abode in our House as a guest for six weeks, being sickly the while, but it was his intention to serve God and to remain with us: also he was a notable benefactor to the House in his lifetime and at his death; and he died in peace in the sixty-eighth year of his age, being fortified by the sacraments of the church. He was buried in the tomb of his mother, Swane ten Water, beneath a sarcophagus of stone that standeth in our church before the Altar of Holy Cross.

In the same year, on the last day of August, and within the Octave of the Feast of St. Augustine, before Matins, died the humble and devout Laic, John Bobert, being forty years old. He came from the diocese of Treves, and formerly was our shepherd, but afterward he became porter to the monastery, and he was very faithful and pitiful to the poor. Having fulfilled twelve years in this House, he fell asleep in peace, and was laid in the burial-ground of the Lay folk.

In the same year, during Advent, on the Octave of the Feast of St. Andrew the Apostle, and before Prime, died an aged man named Gerard Poelman. He was a Donate of our House, and was born in Zwolle, but he lived with us for sixty-two years, having come to us in the days when we were still very poor, and lacked goods, buildings, books, and holy vestments. His parents often succoured us and did us much kindness, for they were somewhat wealthy, and they gave or lent us money to buy provision, because they loved their sons who dwelt with us, namely, Henry, and this Gerard that was the younger brother. These two had one sister, whose name was Adelaide, a devout virgin, who for many years ruled over the House of the Béguines at Nyerstadt, where at length she died amid the nuns, and she was buried by the Brothers of the Regular Order in Bethlehem.

At first this Gerard was the tailor of our monastery, as was also his brother Henry, but afterwards he faithfully discharged the duty of fisherman, but when weakness compelled him to abandon this task, he became the gardener, and was skilful in growing vegetables and herbs of divers kinds. At last, wearied with years and overborne with toil, he fell asleep in a good old age, for he was eighty-one years old, and in return for his labours received a crown of life at the hands of the King of Glory. He was laid in the burial-ground of the Laics and servants of the House, on the western side of our church, and the venerable, devout, and holy Father George performed the rites.

In the year 1463, on the day before the Feast of Quirinus the Martyr, that is on March 29th, and at about the eighth hour when Compline was done, died John, son of James, a faithful Laic of our House and a good husbandman; he was an Oblate and Resignate, and was born in Dalssen; moreover, he proved himself to be useful and skilled in his work among our husbandmen. He was well beloved, and lived in this monastery for twenty-eight years, but having fulfilled forty-six years of life, he departed in holy peace, and was buried near Gerard Poelman, in the burial-ground of the Laics, on the Wednesday before Palm Sunday.

In the same year, on the 15th of May, being the fifth Sunday after Easter, and the third day after the Feast of Servatius, three young Clerks were invested, namely, Peter, son of Simon, of Liege, William, son of Peregrinus, of Kampen, and Arnold Wanninck of Deventer, own brother to Theodoric Wanninck of our community. Brother Peter, the first of these, was twenty-three years old; the second, namely, William, was twenty-one; and Arnold Wanninck, the younger, was twenty. At their investiture our Father George performed the ceremony and celebrated High Mass of the Resurrection.

In the year 1464, on the 15th of May, being the Tuesday after the Feast of the Ascension of our Lord, Hubert, son of Nicholas, of Amersfoort, who was thirty-five years old, was invested as a Convert of our House. For some years he had been town crier, and he was well beloved, being a trusty friend to the devout Brothers and Sisters in their business. When his wife was dead and his sons had received their portions, he chose to leave the world and humbly to serve God in the monastery; so after a probation of nearly three years he was invested solemnly as a Convert.

In the same year, and on the day following the Feast of St. James the Apostle, died Andrew, son of Hermann, of Sichele, a faithful and devout Laic of our House and an Oblate to God. He had no possessions of his own, nor did he leave behind him any private store, no not one mite. He came to our monastery on the Feast day of St. Agnes, in the year of the Lord 1419, being then twenty-one years old; and having fulfilled with us in the service of God nearly forty-four years, being then sixty-five years of age, he departed from this world. His death came about through a sudden mischance, for having fallen from a horse, he was hurt grievously, and commending himself to God, he fell asleep in holy faith and peace. And he was laid in the burial-ground of the Laics.

In the same year, on the Feast day of St. Matthew, Apostle and Evangelist, there fell a great tempest of wind, and many trees were broken and torn from the earth; likewise large ships were sunk in the sea, and in many parts, as also at Rome, the pestilence raged so that a great multitude of men that had thought to live long died thereof.

In the year of the Lord 1465, on the Feast of the Annunciation of the Blessed Virgin Mary, a young Clerk named Reyner Koetken was invested. He was nineteen years of age, and sprung from an honourable stock, having good parents and friends at Zwolle: moreover, he had three sisters who were living the Religious Life as Béguines in the House of Wyron that lieth near the city without the northern gate.

In the same year, in the month of March, and during the Lenten season, God succoured our House by granting us to catch a great number of fishes in the river Vecht, which is near the monastery, and these sufficed for all that dwelt with us, and likewise for the poor, and for strangers; also many traders came from the regions of Westphalia and Saxony to buy these fish which are called smelts.

In the same year a new monastery was founded in Zwolle for the Order of Preachers.

In the same year, in the month of July, and on the day before the Feast of St. Praxedes the Virgin, died our beloved Brother Henry Lymborgh, a Priest, who was born in Zwolle. He was fifty years old, and he was buried in the eastern cloister, by the side of Henry, son of William, our fourth Prior. Often he fell sick with the stone, and at the end, having fulfilled twenty-seven years in the Religious Life, he had a slight stroke of palsy in the face, and he fell asleep in peace amongst the Brothers. In the same year, in the month of October, and on the day following the Feast of St. Michael the Archangel (that is, the night of the Feast of St. Leodegarius, Bishop and Martyr), died John Tyman, a native of Holland. He was a faithful Laic and an Oblate, and when he finished his course was seventy years of age.

For forty-five years he lived with us humbly, and in obedience working with the husbandmen, albeit for a long time he had been lame; and after a long trial by sickness he rendered up his soul with patience, and was laid in the western burying-ground with the other Laics.

In the same year, and on the day before the Feast of the holy Martyrs, Crispin and Crispian, one Bernard Irte died at Zwolle, being a citizen of that city, and son of Lambert of Irten, a magistrate of the State. He was a friend to our House, and during his lifetime often visited our church, in which out of his devotion to St. Agnes the Virgin he desired to be buried, and he was laid with the Converts in the western cloister before the door of the church.

In the year 1466, on the night of the Feast day of St. Maurus the Abbot, and before Matins, died Wolter Eskens, the father of Gerlac, our cellarer; he was an ancient man, being ninety years old, and he had been formerly our husbandman on a certain farm pertaining to the monastery at Windesem, but he was born in the town of Raelten. In his old age he left his friends and acquaintance, following his son Gerlac, who was a faithful Oblate, and he lived in our House for nearly eleven years before his death.

Long had he been bowed with age, yet he hastened to the church every morning to hear Mass, leaning upon a staff. He was very good and patient in bearing his bodily weakness, and he fell asleep in the Lord, giving thanks. So after Mass had been said for him, he was buried with the Laics and servants of our House, in the burying-place of the Donates.

In the same year, on the Octave of the Feast of St. Agnes the Virgin, died Christian, a Priest, who was eighty years old. He was Curate of Ter Heyne, and a special friend to our House, and out of his devotion he chose to be buried with our Brothers, so he was laid in the eastern cloister in the same grave with Hermann Gruter the Priest.

In the year of the Lord 1467, on the third day of the month of March, and before Compline, died Hysbrand, our tailor, a Resignate and Oblate, who was born in Amsterdam, a town of Holland. For thirty years he had lived with us, and he was laid in the burying-place of the Laics, being seventy-two years of age when he died.

In the same year, on the Feast day of the holy Apostles Peter and Paul, died Tidemann Mulart, a native of Hasselt. He was a Resignate and an Oblate, who had long discharged many hard tasks as a servant of our House, for he abode with us for near of forty-four years, and at length he departed in peace, being seventy-two years old, and he was laid in the burying-place of the Laics.

In the same year the Brothers and members of the House at Windesem builded and enlarged their ancient church to promote the honour of God.

In the same year, after the Feast of Pentecost, our Father George built a new kitchen that was greater and more stoutly wrought than the former, for the old kitchen was roofed with reeds and thatch, and he built this new one by reason of the peril of fire, and also to rid us of certain ill conveniences, and to promote the good of the community.

In the same year, on the night of the Assumption of the Blessed and Glorious Virgin Mary, and after the Te Deum had been sung, died the devout Laic, Nicholas Bodiken, who was an Oblate of our House. He served Christ faithfully, and showed special devotion in singing the praises of the Most Blessed Virgin.

A few days before his death he was seized with grievous pain in the head and his other members, but being purged by this sore suffering in the body, he gained an happy issue therefrom, for his end was such as he would have wished, and he met the same with a good will and with complete resignation on the day aforesaid, which was the solemn feast of the Blessed Virgin.

When supper was ended, Nones of the Blessed Virgin were sung, and Vigils recited for him, and then he was laid in the burying-place of the Laics and amongst the Oblates and Donates of our House; being in the seventy-ninth year of his age when he died. He had lived for a great while with us, but the needs of his mother and grandmother constrained him to take care of them, which thing he did, having taken counsel with the Prior of our House, but after that they died in Zwolle, he returned to the monastery at Mount St. Agnes. After this he fulfilled thirty years in complete subjection to our rule, and on the Feast day aforesaid he fell asleep in the Lord, and all that dwelt in this House bore witness to his good report.

On this same Feast of the Assumption of the Blessed Mary, our most beloved Father George took the Ciborium of the Venerable Sacrament from the altar with all reverence, and the whole body of members, going before him in procession round the cloister, sang the Response, "Felix namque." After they had returned to the choir, they bowed the knee before the Revered Sacrament which was placed upon the altar, and sang the

Antiphon, "Media Vita," with the verse and the Collect proper to times of pestilence, for at this time the plague had begun both here and in many places.

In the same year, by the blessing of God, our orchard bare much fruit, but the fields, though they stood thick with corn, were hurt by the continued rain that fell at harvest time. Wherefore frequent prayers to God for fair weather were made at the time of Mass, and the seven psalms were recited in the choir.

In the same year, on the Feast of St. Simon and St. Jude, died Arnold of Nemel, an aged farmer, who was a neighbour and a good friend to our House. He was laid in the western cloister before the door of the church, and in one grave with his son.

In the same year, after the Feast of All Saints, and after Compline, on the day before the Feast of Leonard the Confessor, died Arnold, son of Gerard of Werendorp, who was our miller, a faithful Laic and Fellow Commoner of our House. He was a man greatly beloved and profitable to the Laics of our household and all the Brothers, and he died after that he had finished the thirty-third year of his age, having continued with us for fourteen years. He was laid in the burying-place of our Laics by the side of Nicholas Bodiken.

In the same year, 1467, Albert, son of Hubert of Amersfoort, was invested on the day of the Conception of the Glorious Virgin Mary, being twenty-three years old, but he had attended the school at Zwolle for four years.

In the year of the Lord 1468, in the month of April, on the day following the Feast of St. Ambrose the Bishop and in the middle of the night, before Lauds, died Godefried Hyselhan of Kampen, a Laic and Donate of our House, being eighty-three years of age. For a great while he was the miller of our monastery, and a man faithful and upright in his conversation. Afterward he became our porter, and showed himself pitiful and kindly to the poor; but at length, worn out with years, he died in peace, for God had mercy on him: and he was laid in the burying-ground of the Laics.

In the year of the Lord 1469, on the day after the Feast of the Holy Innocents—which day is the Feast of St. Thomas of Canterbury, and falleth within the Octave of the Lord's Nativity—died Brother Gerard that was called Cortbeen, whose death befell after supper, and before the hour of Vespers. Before he entered the Religious Life he was a Priest, and he was born at Herderwyjc, but for ten years past he had lived the Religious Life amongst us in piety and devotion. Often he endured much toil in time of harvest, and in winter also he would cut wood in the marshland, for he was a strong man and apt for coarse and heavy toil, yet he neglected not the inner things of God. At the last he was afflicted of the Lord with a dropsy in the legs, and after bearing the scourge of this infirmity he departed out of this world to the Lord in the forty-second year of his age. So Mass and Vigils for the dead were said for him, and he was buried in the eastern cloister.

In the year of the Lord 1470, on the third day after the Feast of Servatius the Bishop, two Clerks, and one Laic who was a Convert, were invested. This was on a week day, so as to avoid the concourse of men, and the gathering together of a crowd of friends from the world.

Of these Clerks the first was Otto Graes of Deventer, who was twenty-two years old and had two brothers living the Religious Life as Priests in the Regular Order: of these one was at Windesem, the other in the House of Bethlehem at Zwolle. The second of the Clerks was Rudolph, son of Gerard, a native of Amersfoort, who was twenty-one years old, and had sojourned for a while at Zwolle before he entered the monastery. The third was Henry Kalker, a Novice and Convert, who came from the region of Kleef, and was thirty-seven years of age: he lived with us before his investiture, dwelling amongst the Laics, and he was a good tailor, but sometimes he served in the kitchen, and sometimes ministered to the sick: after a while, by reason of his uprightness, he was invested as a Convert.

In the same year, on the day following the Feast of the holy Martyr Maurice and his companions, and after Matins had begun, died our Brother Peter Herbort, a Deacon who was sixty-five years old. He was of weak frame, and by nature very frail, so that he was unable to observe many of the statutes, yet he often received discipline in the Chapter for his faults: also he washed the heads of the Brothers when they were shaven, and rejoiced to serve the others as reader in the Refectory. At length, having fulfilled forty-three years in the habit of the Regular Order, the time came for him to go forth; so being contrite of heart, having made his confession and received the Communion and the Unction, he fell asleep in the Lord in good confidence and faith amid the prayers of the Brothers. For our Father George, with many of the Brothers, was present with him, but the rest remained in the choir to sing Matins and Lauds. After supper Vigils were sung for him and for our other benefactors, and he was buried in the eastern cloister by the side of our Brother Gerard Cortbeen.

In the year of the Lord 1471, that is to say, on the Feast day of Antony the Confessor, and in the morning after High Mass, died that devout Laic, Gerlac, son of John, who was born hard by Zwolle, that is to say, at Dese. He was seventy-two years old, and for the last fifty-three years and more had lived with us in great humility, simplicity, and patience. He bore many toils and privations, and amongst the other virtues that he showed, he was especially notable for the virtue of silence, so that through all the day he spoke but very little, and even during the hours of toil he gave an example of silence to others.

A short while before his death he was smitten with apoplexy, and became partly delirious and he was laid in our burying-ground with the rest of the Laics.

SO FAR THE CHRONICLE WAS WRITTEN BY THOMAS OF KEMPEN; THE RESIDUE THEREOF WAS DONE BY ANOTHER.

In the same year, on the Feast of St. James the Less, and after Compline, died our most beloved Brother Thomas Hemerken, who was born in the city of Kempen, in the diocese of Cologne. He was in the ninety-second year of his age, and this was the sixty-third year after his investiture; likewise he had been a Priest for above fifty-seven years.

In the days of his youth he was an hearer of Florentius at Deventer, by whom also he was sent, when twenty years old, to his own brother, who at that time was Prior of Mount St. Agnes. From this same brother he received his investiture after six years of probation, and from the early days of the monastery he endured great poverty and many labours and temptations.

Moreover, he wrote that complete copy of the Bible which we use, and also many other books for the use of the House, and for sale. Likewise he composed divers little books for the edification of the young, which books were plain and simple in style, but mighty in the matter thereof and in their effectual operation.

The thought of the Lord's passion filled his heart with love, and he was wondrous comfortable to the troubled and the tempted; but as age grew upon him he was vexed with a dropsy in the legs, and so fell asleep in the Lord and was buried in the eastern cloister by the side of Brother Peter Herbort. In the same year, on the Feast day of St. Lambert, and after Prime, Brother Hermann Craen the Vestiarius died of the plague, being sixty-four years old. In the beginning he was Sacristan, but afterward, and for above fifteen years, Vestiarius. Then for thirteen years he held the office of Procurator, but being set aside from that office, he was for the second time appointed to be Vestiarius, in which vocation he gained much praise for that he provided sufficiently for every man so far as the means of the House did allow. After that he was set aside from his office of Procurator he bore himself patiently: and he had lived the Religious Life with us for thirty-eight years and a half: but in the day aforesaid, when Vigils had been sung for him, he was buried after supper-time in the eastern passage.

In the same year, on the day before the Feast of St. Francis, and after Matins, Wichman Spuelre died of the plague. He was a young Laic about twenty-five years of age who was born at Doesborgh, but for above four years he had lived with us; and being chosen to be Sub-Infirmarius he served the sick with kindliness and in gracious wise, wherefore he obtained great praise from all men. He was laid in the burial-ground of the Laics, but on the day following, namely, on the Feast of St. Francis, and just before one o'clock, three Priests and one Lay Brother were anointed with the oil of the sick. In the same year, on the day after the Feast of St. Francis, Brother Henry, son of Paul of Mechlin, who was a Priest, died of the plague. He was nearly forty-six years of age, and was Infirmarius, in which same office he had served the Brothers faithfully for fifteen years; but he had lived with us in the Religious Life for twenty-four years and a half, and he was buried in the eastern cloister beneath the steps, and in the same tomb with Nicholas Creyenscot, who died before.

It is told of this Brother, as an ensample and memorial of him, that on the third day after that he was smitten with the plague, seeing that sure sign of death which is vulgarly called the "Death Spot," and while his strength of mind and body were yet whole in him, he asked for the habit to be brought wherein, after the custom of the Order, he must be buried; and when it was given him he put it on without help from another, and with his own hand sewed up the forepart thereof lest others might unwittingly look upon his body. Then after supper-time was ended, he, with the Infirmarius who was acting for him, read the Litanies and the seven penitential psalms for all his negligences;

and as an act of gratitude for all the benefits that God had bestowed upon him, he added the Te Deum Laudamus. So at length, about the hour of Vespers, having made a good confession, he rendered up his soul, Father George being there present with him, while the Brothers were singing the verses antiphonally in the choir.

In the same year, on the Feast of St. Marcus the Pope, when dinner was ended, Peter, son of Nicholas, a Laic of our household, died of the plague. He was born in Amsterdam, and was about fifty years old, but he had lived with us for twenty-five years and a half, being employed in the brewery. He was a strong man of great stature, and a pattern to the Laics by reason of his close observance of the habit of silence, his regularity in reading the Vigils, frequenting the church, and such like exercises. He was laid in the burial-ground of the Laics.

In the same year, on the day following the Feast of St. Dionysius the Martyr, and before the ninth hour in the evening, Brother Peter, son of Simon, who was born in Liège, died of the plague; now he had lived with us in the Religious Life for nine years and a half. By nature he was very timid and modest, and at the beginning of his conversion he had suffered many temptations to cowardice, albeit he was afterwards delivered from these by the grace of God. So he yearned for death with great desire, longing to be released and to be with Christ, and he was laid in the eastern cloister.

In the same year, on the day following the Feast of St. Luke the Evangelist, and after Matins, Peter, son of John, died of the same plague. He was a Laic and Resignate of about seventy-three years of age, who was born in Utrecht; but he had lived with us for about fifty-four years, and was employed in binding books. By nature he was very weakly, especially in the head, and he often received discipline for his negligences, being punished therefore: yet he did gladly serve for the Brothers at Mass, and at the last, in the time of the plague, he got his death through ministering to the sick, and died in the presence of Father George, and was laid with the other Laics in their burying-ground.

In the same year, on the day following the Feast of the Eleven Thousand Virgins, and in the morning after Prime, died our Brother John Kysendael, who was born at Orsoy in the land of Kleef. He was almost thirty-four years old, and had lived with us in the Religious Life for fourteen years and nearly two months, being much beloved for his holy conversation and his virtuous life. Moreover, he served the Brothers humbly in his office of sacristan for nearly four years, and so that versicle which is sung for confessors was apt and fitting for him "who was ever pious and prudent, lowly and modest, sober and chaste and peaceful so long as this present life endured in his bodily limbs." He was buried in the eastern cloister.

Two hours afterwards, on the same day, and of the same plague, died Hermann Crom, a Laic and Resignate, who was born in Utrecht, being now sixty-four years old, but he had lived with us for nearly thirty-four years; he was of great service to the Brothers, first in the office of Sub-Infirmarius, and afterward in making ready the Refectory and ministering to the other needs of those Brothers that were weak and old. At length, as he served the sick, he was smitten with the plague, and was laid in the burying-ground of the Laics.

In the same year, on the Feast of St. Simon and St. Jude, and after supper-time, Laurentius died of this same plague. He was a Laic and Donate, and his native place was Alsen, a town near Tyel in the parts of Geldria. He was seventy-three years of age, and had been barber to the House, having lived with us for near forty-five years. A great company of strangers resorted to him hoping to be cured by his skill as a surgeon, for he had some good knowledge of that art. He was laid in the burying-place of the Laics.

In the same year, on the Feast of St. Martin the Bishop, and before the tenth hour in the evening, Ludolph the miller died of the plague. He was born at Delden in Twenthe, and was nearly thirty-seven years old, but he had lived with us for three years and a half. He fell sick through tending the plague-stricken, for he was at this time their faithful servant; and having made a good confession, and being filled with a fervent love of God, he died and was laid in the burying-ground of the Laics.

In the year of the Lord 1472, on the Feast day of St. Ambrose, which fell on the Sunday after Easter, died Brother Everard ter Huet, a native of Zwolle, and Prior at Bergum, where for ten years and more he had ruled the Brothers in laudable wise. Having fulfilled forty-three years of life, twenty-five of which he had passed as a member of our Order, he died at last, being smitten with the plague, and was buried in the church of the aforesaid monastery.

In the same year, on the fourth day after the Feast of St. Ambrose, and when Prime was done, died our Brother John Lent that was a native of a place near Zwolle, being nearly eighty years old; but he had lived with us in the Religious Life for about fifty-nine years. He was very strict in his observance of the rule, and a pattern to the Brothers, but at length, being worn out with the disease called stone, he died, and was buried in the eastern cloister. By his writing he was of much profit to the monastery, for he attained great excellence in this art, wherefore he wrote many books for sale, and many for the choir and the libraries, wherein he left a notable example for others to imitate.

In the same year, on the day of St. Potentiana the Virgin (which was the Tuesday after Pentecost), and when Vespers were done, Johson of Tric died of a rupture. He was a Laic and Resignate, a native of Zwolle, and seventy-five years old; but he had lived with us for fifty-one years, being a pattern to the Laics by the toils that he bore, and his obedience to discipline. By reason of his trustiness he was often set over the husbandmen at Lunenkerc at the time of our exile, and also at home, that is, at Mount St. Agnes. But at the last he died suddenly and without making confession, for death was beforehand with him; howbeit he received the Unction, and he had made his confession two days before he died, and had received Communion with the others on the Feast of Pentecost.

In the same year, on the fourth day after the Feast of St. Lucia, died Gherard, son of Hermann, a Laic of our household, who was born near Albergen in Twenthe. He was nearly fifty years old, and had lived with us for twenty-three years. His stature was small, but his mind great, and he directed our husbandry with all diligence; but at length he fell into a consumption owing to a kick from a horse, and having lingered a long while, he died, and was laid in the burying-ground of the Laics.

In the year of the Lord 1473, on the 28th day of June, two Brothers were invested as Clerks. The first was Stephen Putselaer, who was born at Doesborgh, and had attended the school at Deventer; he was now twenty-two years old. The second was John, son of Tric, a native of Amsterdam, who had sojourned at the school of Zwolle for nearly four years, and at the time of his investiture he was at the beginning of his eighteenth year.

In the year of the Lord 1474, on the day before the Feast of St. Agatha, Virgin and Martyr, and in the morning between the sixth and seventh hours, died Brother Otto Lyman, a native of Goch, being nearly seventy-six years old, but he had lived with us for fifty-five years and a little more. He was very zealous for discipline, and most strict in observing the rule of silence; also it was his custom to attend all the services in the church, each in its season, so much so that although weakened by old age and an apoplexy, he did not forgo this custom to the very end of his life. Besides this he carefully observed a voluntary poverty both in the matter of his clothing and with regard to the furniture of his cell. During his life he wrote many books for the library; but at length his infirmities grew upon him, and he fell asleep in the Lord in the presence of the venerable Prior and the Brothers, and was buried in the eastern cloister.

In the year of the Lord 1474, on the day of St. Urban, Bishop and Martyr, brother Martin, son of Nicholas, was invested. He was nineteen years of age and was born at Amsterdam, but he had attended the school of Brussels for three years.

In the year of the Lord 1474, on the second day after the Feast of the Conception of the Virgin Mary, and after Matins, died Brother Theodoric Veneman, who was born near Zwolle, being now seventy-two years old; but he had lived a laudable life with us for fifty-two years, lacking two months. He was of ripe character and a pattern Brother; moreover, he was zealous in observing the rule of silence and quietness, but at length he fell sick and slept in the Lord, and the venerable Prior George and the Brothers were with him at his death. He was buried in the eastern cloister.

In the year of the Lord 1474, on the day of St. Agapitus the Martyr, died Goswin ter Beeck, a Laic of our household, who was born in Zwolle, being -- years old, but he had lived with us for about fifty-three years; his life was a very pattern, and well ordered, both in word and deed; he had been our miller for more than forty years, and was very faithful to the House. In that he greatly feared that death should come suddenly, he made his confession to the venerable Prior after due preparation, and a short time afterwards he met that death which he had feared, for God ordained it so.

In the same year died our beloved Brother Gerard, son of Tric, that was a Convert. This befell on the second day after the Feast of St. Lucia, Virgin and Martyr, and after Matins. He was eighty-two years old, and for many years had been a Donate, but having lived honestly amongst us for more than thirty years he was invested as a Convert, for so it seemed good to the Prior and the whole Brotherhood. He was most strict in observing discipline, weighty in word and character, austere toward himself, and a lover of poverty. Moreover, he directed our husbandry, and that of two other Houses of our Order, to wit, the Houses at Anyhen and at Lunenkerc, also that of the monastery belonging to the Order of St. Benedict which is called the House of Kleerwater, near Hattem; for out of charity to the Brothers of that House the venerable Prior lent Gerard to them. So having lived with us for nearly fifty-four years in this honest and devout wise, he fell asleep in the Lord and was buried in the western passage which is called "The Strangers' Passage," together with the other Converts.

In the year 1475, on the fourth day after the Feast of Maurice and his companions, and about the fifth hour in the morning, died William Brant, a Laic of our household, but a Clerk in regard to learning. He was born at Kampen, and was now nearly seventy-five years old; but he had lived with us for nearly sixty years. Although he was notable for knowledge, yet he desired to continue humbly, modestly, and in quietness unto his life's end in the condition of a Laic, and specially to avoid the sin of detraction. Beside his unceasing labours in other matters, he awakened the Brothers for Prime during forty years.

In the year 1473, on the third day after the Feast of St. Matthias the Apostle, and in the morning, died Encbert of Tyveren, a Donate and Fellow Commoner of our House, being eighty-three years old. Amongst other virtuous habits, he had one that is specially worthy to be remembered, namely, that if any did him a wrong, he would easily and without hesitation grant full forgiveness for the same, whenever the offender showed any sign of charity toward him. Being fired, moreover, with charity and love for God and his neighbour, and with a zeal for souls that ceased not night or day, he strove for their good whenever he had opportunity; and of this many can bear witness, both men and women, for whom he obtained places fit for them wherein they might serve God.

In the same year and week, namely, on the fifth day after the Feast of St. Matthias, John Bodien (?) died at Deventer. He was a Laic of our household, and being oppressed by infirmity he went to Deventer to take counsel of a physician, and there died in his brother's house; and since he was born of a good stock, his body was brought back to us with honour by his friends, and laid in the burying-ground of the Lay folk. For a few years after his conversion he served in the kitchen, and coming to his life's end he fulfilled the toils of many years in a short space.

In the year of the Lord 1477, on the Octave of the Feast of the visitation of the Blessed Mary, and after Nones, that is at about the eighth hour, died Gerlac, son of Wolter. He was a devout man and very trusty; a Laic and Resignate that was born at

Ralt, and he was nearly seventy-one years old. On the day before his death, and after Compline, he took his supper in the kitchen according to his custom (for he was cellarer) and by a mysterious visitation of God he suddenly was deprived of all sense and strength. He lost the power of speech, and he lay until next day struck down with apoplexy without speaking or eating, and died after Nones at the hour aforesaid. He had lived with us for nearly forty years, during twenty-three of which he had fulfilled the duties of the aforesaid office with faithfulness and care, being almost always in his cell and ready to carry out the wishes of the Brothers. He was laid with the other Laics in that burying-ground of ours that pertains to them of that condition.

In the same year, on the Feast of St. Ægidius, and after Compline, that is to say about the middle of the seventh hour, died that devout Laic, Albert, son of Florentius. He was a Resignate and about seventy-three years old, but he had lived with us for nearly forty-five years, and for a long while served the Brothers patiently in the kitchen. But afterwards he was very serviceable to the sick, and to the Infirmarius, by catching and bringing them fresh fish. He was laid with the others in the burying-ground of the Laics.

FROM THE CHRONICLE OF OUR BROTHER THOMAS OF KEMPEN CONCERNING MATTERS NOT PERTAINING TO OUR HOUSE.

CHAPTER I.

Concerning the year in which that reverend man, Florentius of Wevelichoven, was made Bishop of Utrecht.

In the year of the Lord 1479, Florentius of Wevelichoven, aforetime Bishop of Munster, was enthroned as Bishop of the Church of Utrecht on the Festival of St. Willibrord, first Bishop of that See.

He was a prudent man of honest life, ripe age, and a lover of religion, and under his rule, which was during the reign of our Lord Pope Urban VI, Gerard Groote flourished, that venerable master who was truly great by reason of his life, his learning, and the words of his preaching.

CHAPTER II.

Of the death of John Ruesbroeck, first Prior of the Groenendaal.

In the year of the Lord 1381, and on the second day of December, being the Octave of St. Katherine, Virgin and Martyr, the venerable and most devout Master John Ruesbroeck died in the district of Brabant. He was the first Prior of the Monastery of the Groenendaal near Brussels, which Monastery pertains to the Order of Canons Regular; he was then in the eighty-eighth year of his age, and he was buried before the north end of the High Altar in the choir. He took the Religious habit in the aforesaid place amongst the first who were there invested, being then sixty years of age; and, by the help of God, he fulfilled the office of the Priesthood for sixty-four years. His holy and glorious doctrine was published far and wide over the land of Germany, and giveth light thereto. This was he whom Master Gerard Groote visited, together with John, a scholar from Zwolle, for he thought that his writings were worthy to be compared with those of the greatest doctors. Moreover, he had put forth many books that were most devout, touching matters of the higher understanding, which books, of his wisdom, he wrote in the Teutonic tongue; and he poured forth in liberal abundance that grace of heavenly sweetness which he had received from God, for the use of his neighbour and them that should come after in the Church. There are eleven books which he composed either before or after his entrance into the Religious Life; and less the tale should be incomplete, the book of his letters doth make that number up to twelve.

There was in the same monastery, under this venerable Master, a Convert whose name was John, a man very devout, who did humbly devote himself to his life's end to serving in the kitchen, and he was illumined with special grace for divine contemplation. He compiled a great and notable book, filled with high and heavenly doctrine, in the which he doth commend his most beloved father, John Ruesbroeck, in most excellent wise.

In the same monastery also were certain other most devout Fathers and Religious Brothers, eminent for their life and wisdom, as their holy works that have come down to us do testify.

Concerning the life and writings of John Ruesbroeck and Brother John Cocus, more is told in a little book that hath been put forth of late, and that is entitled "Of the Origin of the Monastery of the Groenendaal."

CHAPTER III.

Of the death of the venerable Master Gerard Groote, a man most devout.

In the year of the Lord 1384, on the Feast day of the blessed Bernard the Abbot, and at the fifth hour, after Vespers, Gerard, surnamed Groote, died at Deventer, in the time of the pestilence; he was a venerable man and beloved of God, and the forty-fourth year of his age was nearly done.

His body was borne to the Parish Church of the most Blessed Virgin, Mother of God, and therein was laid with due honour not far from the sanctuary. His father's name was Werner Groote, and he was a Schepen and magistrate of the same city; his mother was called Heylwige, and both her husband and she were of high place and mighty in honour and riches, judged after the measure of worldly dignity; but Gerard, by God's inspiration, put aside the burden of riches and despised the pomps of the world on the which he had relied carelessly for a long while, and for the sake of an humble Christ took upon him a garb of humility. Suddenly he was changed into another man, so that all wondered, and he became a rule of life to Clerks and Lay folk alike. Hereafter, by the pattern of his good conversation and the exhortation of his holy preaching, he withdrew many persons from the vanities of the world and laid upon them the gentle yoke of Christ. Likewise he resigned all his ecclesiastical benefices, but he kept some small portion of his father's goods to provide for his own necessities. Much he gave to the Religious, and his dwelling-house and homestead lie bequeathed for ever to the poor Sisters, or Béguines, whom he had gathered together in that same place. Of his humility he took upon him the rank of a deacon so that he might be able to preach, but he would not take priestly orders because of the awe in which he held the same.

On a time he went toward Zwolle in company with Peter, Curate of the Church of Deventer, and his companion questioned him with friendly boldness, saying: "Beloved Master, why wilt

thou not be made Priest, since thou art well lettered and fitted to rule others?" But Gerard made answer: "I would not be Curate of Zwolle, no, not for a single night, for my cap full of golden florins." And Peter being astonished said: "What then shall we feeble and wretched folk do, for our knowledge and our life are less worthy than thine?" And this word of Master Gerard had so great weight that this same Peter did afterward renounce his pastoral charge and did maintain himself upon a single benefice, and that one to which no cure was attached. Gerard, moreover, wrote profitable treatises, and many letters to divers persons, and from these writings one may see readily enough how great a zeal for souls was in him, and how deep an understanding of the Scriptures. He translated two books of John Ruesbroeck from the Teutonic into the Latin tongue, and these are entitled: "Ecce Sponsus" and "De gradibus amoris." Likewise he translated "The Hours of the Blessed Virgin," and certain of the Hours from the Latin into the Teutonic tongue, so that simple and unlearned Laics might have in their mother tongue matter wherewith to occupy themselves in prayer on holy days; and also that the faithful, reciting these Hours, or hearing them recited by other devout persons, might the more readily keep themselves from many vanities and from idle talking, and so, being assisted by these holy readings, might make progress in the love of God and in singing the divine praises. Once a certain man who was united to him in the bonds of friendship, asked him, saying: "Most beloved Master, of what use are all these books which you carry on so great journeys?" And Gerard answered: "For good living a few books are enough; but we must have all these for the instruction of others and to defend the truth, so that if any might not believe me yet they may assent to the authority of the saints."
Many other good things also Master Gerard did in his life, as certain worthy records of him tell us, so that from the small band of his disciples there grew at length a great company of devout persons.

CHAPTER IV.

Of the great eulogy passed upon Gerard by a certain doctor.

Master Gerard of holy memory, he who was called "The Great," has passed happily to the Lord. Truly he was "The Great," for in his knowledge of all the liberal sciences, both natural and moral, of civil law, canon law, and of theology, he was second to no one in the world, and all these branches of learning were united in him.

He was a man of such saintliness and gave so good an example in his mortification of the flesh, his refusal of temporal advantages, his contempt for the world, his brotherly love for all, his zeal for the salvation of souls, his effectual preaching, his reprobation and hatred of wickedness, his withstanding of heretics, his enforcement of the canon law against those that broke the vow of chastity, his conversion to the spiritual life of divers men and women who had formerly lived according to the world, and his loyalty to our Lord Urban the Sixth—in all those things I say he gave so good an example, that many thousands of men testify to the belief that is in them that he was not less great in these virtues than he was in the aforesaid sciences. Master William of Salvarvilla, Cantor at Paris, Archdeacon of Brabant in the Church of Liège, an eminent doctor in theology, compiled the above eulogy from that which he heard from the lips of men worthy of credit, and from his own knowledge of Master Gerard, and he believed beyond all doubt that it was true.

CHAPTER V.

How, after his death, the number of the Devout and the Order of Regulars did increase.

After the death of the venerable Master Gerard Groote, the devotion of faithful persons in Deventer, Zwolle, Kampen and the neighbouring towns began to grow mightily in the Lord, so that in a short time there arose many congregations of men and women that served God, dwelling together in common and in chastity of life after the manner of the primitive Church and that laudable custom of the holy Fathers that was introduced by the Apostles.

Some of these who could ill abide the concourse of people in the cities, sought habitations that did befit them far from the places where men do congregate, and having builded them poor little houses, determined to lead a hidden life therein after the example of the ancient Fathers; but in process of time, as their numbers and their goods increased, they took upon them the habit of holy religion, for God so ordered it, and converted their houses into Monasteries of the Order of Canons Regular, thinking thereby to be the more profitable. This same memorable Master, inspired with a spirit of prophecy, foretold this thing, namely, that the number of the devout should increase mightily, for to a certain Priest, who was his friend, and afterward became a Canon Regular at Zwolle (from whom also I heard the saying), he said: "Behold, beloved, this good thing which by God's help hath been here begun, shall be increased yet more, and this little spark shall kindle many fires throughout all Holland and Geldria."

Thanks be to God that as we have heard, so have we seen with our own eyes the fulfilment of this prophecy, and that not only in the regions round about, but also in the parts afar off and in the upper provinces. He had it likewise in mind to found, with the help of certain friends, a monastery for Regulars who should take the habit which he had seen in Brabant in the house of John Ruesbroeck, but this purpose he committed to the followers whom he had made firm in the faith of Christ, that they should fulfil it, for death was beforehand with him, and this was, indeed, fulfilled effectually by these same disciples in after days.

CHAPTER VI.

Of the consecration of the Church, and the investiture of the first Brothers in Windesem.

In the year of the Lord 1387, on the day before the Feast of St. Luke the Evangelist, the first Church of the Monastery in Windesem was consecrated in Honour of the glorious Virgin Mary, Mother of God.

This place received the name Windesem from the village that lieth near to it, and it is one mile from Zwolle, toward the south; near the eastern side thereof is the River Yssel; also some space away is Hattem, the strongest fortress in Geldria.

On this same day six Brothers made their profession and were invested with the habit of the Order of Canons Regular, who observe the rule of Augustine, the glorious Bishop and Father of our Order. The names of these are as followeth:

Brother Henry of Huxaria, a Priest.

Brother Werner of Lochem, in Geldria, the first Prior of the house there.

Brother John of Kempen, in the diocese of Cologne, who was afterward Prior at Mount St. Agnes.

Brother Henry Wilde of Hertzogenbosch, in Brabant.

Brother Berthold ten Hove, a native of Holland, who conveyed to us his patrimony and the place where the monastery standeth.

Brother Henry Wilsem of Kampen, a man of great probity, who was formerly a great one in the world. He was eloquent in discourse, humble and earnest in the service of God.

With these and others that loved holy religion, this new foundation of the Order of Canons Regular in the diocese of Utrecht had its beginning after the happy death of Master Gerard Groote, and under the rule of Florentius, Bishop of Utrecht, it increased by little and little, but in process of time it began to grow yet more fruitfully in divers places. All the men above named, save only one, had been disciples of Master Gerard, by whom they, with many other Clerks, were drawn to the amending of their lives, being imbued with his wholesome exhortation.

CHAPTER VII.

Of the death of John de Gronde, a Priest.

In the year of the Lord 1392, on the 17th day of May, being the day following the Feast of St. John before the Latin Gate, and at the fourth hour in the morning, John de Gronde died at Deventer, in the house of Florentius. He was a devout Priest and a mighty Preacher of the Word, and it was in the fortieth year of his age. The town of Octmesheim, in the district of Twent, and the diocese of Cologne, was his native place, and he was a man adorned with modesty and eloquence, and the venerable Master Gerard let summon him from Amsterdam in Holland to hear the confessions of the devout, likewise Gerard committed to him the governance of the Sisters of his House. For awhile he abode with the first Brothers in the ancient House of Florentius, and rose up with the others in the morning to recite the Hours; and when the time for rising came, he awoke straightway and went forthwith to arouse the other Brothers, knocking and saying: "Arise, watch and pray, that ye enter not into temptation." Of this thing Master Gerard maketh mention in the letter which he wrote to the priests at Amsterdam, what time he besought that John should be sent to him, for this alacrity did especially please him.

As his death drew on, Father Florentius, who earned the love of all the devout, stood by him to comfort and console him; to whom John spake, saying: "Lo! the adversary doth strive to disquiet me, and would confound me at the last." But Florentius answered: "Fear not but trust in the Lord, and keep silence as to those things that are cast up against thee." Then John, as one truly obedient, said: "In the name of the Lord," and these were the last words that he spake before his death. He was buried in the Church of the Blessed Mary, ever Virgin, by the side of Master Gerard and in the same tomb, for it was in this church that he had oft proclaimed aloud the Word of God. Likewise from time to time he would preach at Zwolle and hold colloquy with the Brothers on the mount, urging them to hold with constant mind to the course they had begun. So these two on earth are covered by one stone, and one Stone, that is an heavenly, did make them firm in the true faith; as they loved one another in life, so in death their bodies are not divided.

CHAPTER VIII.

Of the death of the most Reverend Florentius of Wevelichoven, Bishop of Utrecht.

In the year of the lord 1393, on the Feast day of St. Ambrose the Bishop (which in that year was Good Friday), while the Holy Office of the Lord's Passion was being said in the church, our most Reverend Lord Florentius of Wevelichoven, Bishop of Utrecht, departed from the light of the world. He died in the city of Hardenberch, having ruled his diocese for twelve years and five months in laudable and glorious wise, and his body was taken to the Church of the Blessed Martin at Utrecht, and was buried with honour in the choir beneath the steps of the sanctuary. Here a taper is kept lighted as a memorial of his good reputation, for verily he was a lover of the true light, and a defender of his country. In discipline he was very strict; and spent naught needlessly or to any unprofitable end, but all that was justly owed he paid honestly, repaying loans, restoring buildings that were decayed, setting up new ones, fortifying towns and castles. He loved the things of God and prudently disposed of worldly matters; by his servants he was beloved, to the poor he was pitiful; he cherished all devout persons, and was accepted of Clerks and people.

CHAPTER IX.

How Frederick of Blanckenhem was chosen to be Bishop.

In the same year, the noble and famous Lord Frederick of Blanckenhem, formerly Bishop of Strasburg, was chosen to the See of Utrecht and confirmed by the authority of the Apostolic See. He was one of lofty mind, famous for knowledge and prudence, and by the help of God he ruled the diocese for many years with great glory, and guarded his country by his victorious might. Beneath his rule the Order of Canons Regular and the devout multitude of Brothers and Sisters spread far and wide, and rejoiced in their prosperity in all regions that lay beneath his jurisdiction.

In this year also three monasteries were founded in Holland, near Amsterdam. One belonging to the Carthusian Order, one to the Canons Regular, and one to the nuns of that same order: this last lieth within the city and near the ditch.

CHAPTER X.

How the monastery at Northorn was founded.

In the year of the Lord 1394, about the time of the Feast of the Purification of the Blessed Virgin Mary, the Clerks belonging to the household and congregation of that venerable Priest, Master Everard of Almelo, a Bachelor in Physic or Medicine, began to prepare a place for a monastery; for of their own free will and by his council they had determined to build an house in Vrensueghen upon an hereditament that is called Enoldint. So having obtained license from that Reverend Lord Otto ten Hoye, Bishop of Munster, and having the consent of the Dean, Archdeacon, and Chapter, which was given on the 1st day of May, a small Oratory was consecrated in this same place during the Advent following and on the Feast day of St. Thomas the Apostle. This Oratory stood where now the church is builded, and there on this same day four Priests of the household of Everard were invested with the habit of the Order of Canons Regular; they were admitted by Wenomar, Bishop of Sebale, a member of the third Order, and Vicar-General for Pontifical Acts to Otto, the Reverend Bishop of Munster: now the names of the Brothers by him admitted are these:

The first was Henry Kyndeshof of Deventer, and there were also Herpe of Lippe, Hermann Plectenberrich, and John of Julich. Of these Hermann Plectenberrich was chosen to be the first Prior, and the four abode by themselves under the authority of the Bishop of Munster, because their founders would not have them subject to any other, but in the year of the Lord 1400 they were placed under the authority of the Chapter-General of Windesem, which is in the diocese of Utrecht, and lieth near Zwolle, as it were one mile distant.

CHAPTER XI.

Of the death of that most devout Priest Florentius, Vicar of the Church of Deventer.

In the year of the Lord 1400, on the day before the Feast of the Annunciation of the Blessed Mary ever Virgin, and when it was now late, and the Ave Maria had rung, there died in his own House at Deventer the Priest Florentius Radewin. He was a man of holy life and the beloved Father of all the devout, an humble Vicar of the Church at Deventer, a Master of the University of Prague, and he was now in the fiftieth year of his age. He was born at Leerdam that is subject to the Count of Arkel, but when he heard of the fame of Master Gerard, he left his native land and became his devout follower and disciple, and in a short space he was a Father to many devout persons, and the first founder of the congregation of Clerks in Deventer.

His garb was simple and gray in colour, his bearing was composed, his bodily presence full of grace, and his aspect lovable. His hair was black, but his beard somewhat gray; his face was thin and had but little colour, his forehead was bald and his gait and bearing were full of dignity.

Once he came on a visitation to Mount St. Agnes, and the Brothers were glad at his coming, and the elder amongst them asked him to deliver some discourse, so he spoke a few words to them on humility and charity, and at the end he added: "See now, ye may be sickened of these words that ye have heard from me," for he did not think that he could say aught worthy to be heard. Nevertheless he was mighty to comfort the devout, and it was a pleasant thing to see him and hear his words. Also the words wherein he confessed that he was not skilled to speak were received as very edifying, and some of the Religious wrote what he said on their tablets and in their books.

This most holy man of God flourished in the days of that venerable Lord Florentius of Wevelichoven and the illustrious Frederick of Blanckenhem, the two famous Bishops of Utrecht.

When his death was announced to them of the city, the Canons and Clerks came together to attend the burying of so great a man, and a vast multitude of people followed as far as to the Church of St. Lebuin, wherein he was buried before the altar he had served, which is dedicated in honour of St. Paul. His life that was adorned with virtue is more fully set forth in the DIALOGUS NOVITIORUM.

CHAPTER XII.

Of the death of Everard of Eza, a Curate in Almelo and a great master of Physic.

In the year of the Lord 1404, on the first day of the month of April, died that reverend man Everard of Eza, the Curate of Almelo and a great master in physic. He often gave the benefits of his healing art without price to many that were sick, but especially to the poor. Likewise he founded and in a special way provided for the Monastery of the Blessed Virgin in the Wood near Northorn, in the Countship of Benthem, and he procured that some of the Clerks who lived with him should be invested there. Amongst physicians he had a great reputation; of the nobles he was honoured, by worldlings he was feared, by the religious he was beloved, and for a long while his fame was good in the land. Moreover, he had been a close friend to Florentius, the Vicar of the Church at Deventer, and rejoiced to visit him; and he often succoured him in his infirmities and expended anxious care upon him; likewise he said of Florentius that it was a thing above human nature that a man so weak should live so long, unless it were that God preserved him.

But let it not be a marvel to any how it came about that these two reverend Fathers and Masters were thus of one heart in the service of God, for He who brought together the Blessed Peter and Paul to preach in Rome did also unite Florentius and Everard in Deventer, to be as it were two bright lights in the world, to dwell together as Brothers like minded in the House and there to comfort themselves and others.

But the conversion of this reverend Master Everard came about after this manner, and was brought by the co-operation of God to an wholesome effect. When the venerable Master Gerard, of whom mention is made above, was preaching the Word of God to the people outside the walls of Deventer, Everard hastened to come to his preaching, for he had heard Gerard's fame and was puffed up with the wisdom of this world; so he came not of brotherly love, but out of a curious mind, desiring to know whether the Master's teaching was consonant with his fame, for he did not hunger for uprightness but rather would catch him in his talk. Yet he stood not openly among the common and simple folk, but behind a pillar, as one that hideth; and behold Almighty God Who knoweth the heart, neither can any hide from His face, did fill the quiver of the preacher with sharp arrows wherewith in secret he pierced through the heart of this curious hearer, who, being pricked thereby, laid aside all the naughtiness of his former vanity, and became a devout disciple of the preacher. For when the preaching was done, he came near to the man of God, and made known how the Lord had dealt with him by means of the preaching, and how this had befallen him as if the preacher had traversed all the hidden places of his heart and seen all the secrets thereof. So Master Gerard received him and confirmed his charity toward him, and at length Everard became his companion and helper in preaching; but not long after his conversion Master Gerard departed to the Lord. After his departure the old enemy stirred up no small enmity against the devout disciples, but God was present with them, giving to them patience and constancy. Now many of the devout were ignorant of Master Everard's conversion, but he wished to join himself to the disciples of Christ that dwelt in Deventer in the House of Florentius; the Brothers, however, when they saw him were afraid, and began to flee from before his face as lambs from before the wolf, and they gat them into the hidden places of their cells; yea, and Florentius himself was fearful, for he knew not what Everard might mean, who aforetime had been harsh enough and had opposed the devout Brothers.

Everard therefore said to Florentius: "Wherefore do these Brothers flee away?" and he answered: "They know not with what mind thou art come," but Everard said, "I am come to amend my life," and when he was still held in suspicion of Florentius, he said after due thought and protesting his innocency: "If ye will not believe my words, at least believe mine acts—I pray you give me a cell for a season, and prove me therein of what spirit I am."

Therefore they took him and assigned to him a cell where he lived long and was wholly converted; for as once he had gained great knowledge of medicine, so now he received no small light in the law of the Lord and in the holy Scriptures.

After this he accepted the dispensation of God towards him, namely, to be still and attend to his heavenly calling, and also following herein the example of Florentius, to gather together into his own house at Almelo certain Clerks and Lay folk, with whom he lived for many years under due discipline. Moreover, lest they who were so gathered together should be scattered abroad after his death, he began to think of a fit place where they might serve God together, and by His help he found such a place as he desired for the founding of a monastery, and here those Brothers whom he had formerly invested in an humble manner were placed. To them he distributed gifts out of his own substance, namely, gold and silver, books and other things for their use, for building and for needful expenses. As regardeth the foundation of this monastery see above, under the year of the Lord 1394. He was buried in his own church at Almelo, where he had governed his people for many years, and he left a good memorial among the devout whom he cherished and loved as a father. On a time when I attended the school at Deventer, I fell sick, and with such care did he tend me that by the mercy of God a like sickness fell not upon me for many years after.

In the same year, on the Feast day of St. Gregory the Pope, the building of our church was begun by brother John of Kempen, the first Prior.

CHAPTER XIII.

Of the death of the Priest Amilius that succeeded Florentius at Deventer.

In the year of the Lord 1404, on the day before the Feast of St. Barnabas the Apostle, Amilius the Priest died at Deventer; he was a mighty zealot for souls, kindly in feeding the poor, austere to himself, compassionate to the sick, comfortable to the troubled, and he was about thirty-two years of age.

He came from the parts of Geldria near Tyele, and coming to Deventer he attended school there for a while, but when he was amongst the foremost of the students he left the school and clave to Florentius, for it was his desire to serve God. Afterward Florentius procured his promotion to the priesthood, and before his death placed him over the whole congregation, likewise he did commit to his charge the governance of the House as being his beloved disciple. This burden that was laid upon him Amilius undertook with much sorrow, and though he was not minded to disobey the command of so great a Father, yet with weeping eyes, lamentation and sighing, he professed himself unworthy of this preferment; likewise in his secret prayer he mourned bitterly, for he desired rather to have the tasks of the kitchen laid upon him than to be preferred to the honoured post of governing men. For in the kitchen he ever rejoiced in his servitude, being safer therein, and having a good conscience; but in the other office a thousand dangers met him, bringing no small care with them. Yet God did not long delay to answer the prayers and sighs of his humble servant, for his burden on earth endured but a short while, and having fulfilled four years and near to three months in the care of governance, the Lord rewarded his faithful labours with eternal rest. His body was laid in the burying-ground of St. Lebuin the Confessor, near that of Lubbert, a Priest of his own House. There also was John of Viana buried, and there Reyner Haerlem the acolyth and many other devout Brothers and Clerks of the House of Florentius rest in peace. After the death of Amilius,

John Haerlem succeeded as ruler of the House, but he was afterwards chosen to govern the sisters at Zwolle, and Godefred of Wesel filled his place, for the Fathers in their prudence did so ordain it.

CHAPTER XIV.

Of the first investiture of the Sisters of our Order in Diepenvene near Deventer

In the year 1408, on the Feast of St. Agnes the Virgin, the Sisters of the Order of Canons Regular in Diepenvene near Deventer were first invested. This investiture was done by Brother John Huesden, the venerable Prior of Windesem; and there were present also the Prior of the House of the Fount of the Blessed Virgin near Arnheim, Brother John of Kempen, Prior of Mount St. Agnes, and many other devout persons, both men and women, who came together eagerly to be present on so notable a day. So then there was great joy for the heavenly marriage of many devout matrons and virgins; but the sound of much weeping ascended to heaven also. The number of them who took on them the habit and the order that followeth the rule of the Blessed Augustine the Bishop was forty-three, and of these three first made their profession the same day, but the others remained Novices for a year. Many of these Sisters were gathered and brought from Deventer from the house of Master Gerard Groote, after that the numbers there began to be increased, and John Brincerinck governed and guided them for a great while.

CHAPTER XV.

How the monastery in Budiken was reformed.

In the year of the Lord 1409, William van den Berg, Bishop elect of Paderborn, began to reform the monastery at Budiken, transferring it from the rule of Canons Secular to that of Canons Regular; and he published on this occasion the licence for their transference, at the end of which are the words following: "To the honoured John Wael, Prior of the Monastery at Zwolle, that is in the diocese of Utrecht, we do by these presents grant, concede, and allow the privileges hereafter following, namely, that he may attach to the Church and Monastery at Budiken a suitable congregation of men devoted to God, when opportunity doth offer, and that they be under the Order of Canons Regular, conforming to the rule observed in the Monastery at Zwolle so far as the rule there obtaining doth permit. We are led to grant this licence for this special reason, namely, that St. Meynulsus, the founder of this monastery, is believed to have belonged to the Order aforenamed; let the said John Wael therefore set over this same congregation a Prior or Superior as may seem expedient to him."

CHAPTER XVI.

Of the death of Gerard Kalker, a devout Priest, and Rector of the House of Clerks.

In the year of the Lord 1409, on the Vigil of the Nativity of Christ, Gerard Kalker died at Zwolle. He was a devout Priest and Rector of the House of Clerks in the said town, and his age was thirty-six years. The town named Kalker in the district of Kleef was his native place, but when he was attending the school at Zwolle he joined himself to the devout Brothers, and himself became one of their congregation. Afterward he was chosen to dwell in the new House that had been built for a congregation of Clerks by Meynold of Windesem, a rich citizen of Zwolle, and after a while was instituted as Rector of the same House, being held worthy of that office by his Elders. He was one of great stature and innocency of life. In word kindly, in counsel wise, in bearing composed; to the poor compassionate, to strangers courteous, and the citizens loved him; moreover, he burned fervently with divine love to gain the souls of many. He was a zealous follower of Florentius, whom he esteemed with all his heart and loved as his dearest Father; likewise he left behind him many devout Brothers whom he had built up to the highest virtues. He was buried in our monastery at Windesem, and Theodoric Herxen, his disciple, succeeded him as Rector.

CHAPTER XVII.

Of the death of Henry of Gouda, a devout Priest, at Zwolle.

In the year of the Lord 1410, on the day of St. Gregory the Pope, Henry of Gouda died at Zwolle. He was a devout Priest and Confessor to the Sisters in that place, having been of old one of the disciples of Florentius, and he was born in Holland near Schoonhoven. Being learned in the Scriptures he was a mighty preacher, and one that did truly despise the world and its riches; he feared not to reprove the vices of sinners, and in his frequent preaching he strove for the salvation of his neighbours; moreover, he kept a strict watch over his own conscience, and guarded his good reputation and humility of life. On a time, as he was passing through the street in a city that is far away, some boys whom he knew not seized him from behind by his cloak, and mocked him with jests because it was his wont to go clad in very simple attire, and a long sad-coloured cloak, for he seemed to take no thought of any outward thing, nor to desire honour. So being thus entreated and disturbed he looked back and said to himself: "Here ought we to dwell, for at Zwolle they say unto us, 'Sir, sir,' yet what merit do we gain thereby?"

Likewise he came sometimes to Mount St. Agnes, and sought to speak with the Brothers in their cells, and as he was holding converse with a certain one of them, he said, amongst many other good things, "Very good is the life that ye pass here, and the more safe is the road that ye traverse in that ye abide in the cloister afar from the multitude of men. I, who almost every day do traffick with worldlings, what can I learn thereby save the acts of worldly men? I am a man untaught, neither have I knowledge of the life of contemplation, nor do I seek to take hold on lofty matters—but sometimes I can preach in simple words to untaught and common folk—yet henceforth I purpose to amend myself with more diligence, and by God's favour to apply myself to things of greater moment." When he said this, that Brother was greatly edified at the humble words that proceeded from his mouth. It is said also in his preaching he uttered this notable saying: "Why should I say more? Words do beget a multitude of words—and acts beget their kind. The fruit of the Word is its fulfilment in deed."

He was buried in the church at Windesem, where also certain other devout Brothers and Priests do sleep, and after him John Haerlem was preferred to rule over the Sisters in Zwolle, since the well-being of the House so determined it; he was one that was sufficiently skilled in sacred learning, and he had lived long and devoutly in Deventer, and moreover had ruled the House of Florentius for several years.

CHAPTER XVIII.

How the Sisters in Bronope were invested.

In the year of the Lord 1411, on the day of the Conception of the Blessed Virgin Mary, the Sisters of the Order of Canons Regular in Bronope were first invested. This House lieth outside the town of Campen, which town is near the bank of the Yssel where that river runneth down to the sea. This investiture, with indelible and perpetual vows to live the life of the cloister, was conferred by the Reverend Fathers and the Priors of our Order, namely, John Vos of Huesden, Prior of Windesem, and William Vorniken of Utrecht, Prior of Mount St. Agnes near Zwolle. To these the care and visitation of the House, and likewise of the house at Diepenvene that lieth without Deventer, were afterward committed by the General Chapter. But the number of these Sisters who were first invested in this place was fourteen, of whom ten became nuns, and four Converts; and of the ten nuns four did make their profession on the same day; the other six, and the four Converts remained for a year as Novices.

In the year of the lord 1412, a General Chapter was holden and the houses of the nuns at Diepenvene and Bronope were incorporated as members of the said Chapter.

CHAPTER XIX.

The death of Wermbold the Priest.

In the year of the Lord 1413, on the Vigil of Pentecost, being the night of the Festival of Barnabas the Apostle, and at the eleventh hour, died Wermbold, a devout Priest of laudable life who was Confessor to the Sisters of the third Order in the House of St. Caecilia. He came from Holland, from a place near Gouda, and for long had stood as a burning and shining light in the city of Utrecht, enkindling many by the word of his preaching and drawing them to the path of right living by his good example and his wholesome counsel; for he was a zealous lover of the holy Scriptures, and an eloquent preacher to the people, one well beloved for his eminent continency of life, and honoured by great folk. He procured that divers books of sacred theology should be written, and translated divers sayings of the Saints into the Teutonic tongue so as to profit the faithful Lay folk who were earnestly desirous to hear the Word of God. At length, when his pious labours in the service of God had been fulfilled with many trials, the good Lord of His great kindness favoured Wermbold with a most sweet consolation in a vision that was revealed to him. His body was taken for reverent burial to the choir of the Church of St. Caecilia, and the last words he spake as life departed were: "For Thou Lord only hast set me in hope."

CHAPTER XX.

Of the death of John Cele, Rector of the School at Zwolle.

In the year of the Lord 1417, on the ninth day of May, which in that year was the fourth Sunday after Easter, the reverend Master John Cele died at Zwolle in the diocese of Utrecht.

He had ruled the scholars there strictly, being an excellent instructor of youth, a zealous lover of the divine Name, and one that closely attended the choral and other offices of the Church and taught others so. This most faithful man, eminent for his honest life, ruled the school for many years, and with discernment taught many of his pupils to love holy religion and the following after God. What Order that is illustrious for its life or reputation hath not had monks that were his pupils? Although above others the Canons Regular, the Cruciferi, and the Cistercians have gained many adherents to the Order from among his students, and of these some, being endued with the grace of virtue, have become fathers of monasteries and rectors of churches. For the pupils who were under his rule learned from their good Master to despise for Christ's sake the glory of this world that vanisheth away, and that in the whirlpool of this mortal life nothing is better and holier than to spurn the enticements of the world and to fight for the Lord of Heaven. In his days it was a lovely thing to enter the town of Zwolle and to see the chosen multitude of scholars that did attend the school. Who could tell in worthy wise with what fatherly care he strove to instruct all in learning and character, and to the leading of an upright life, and the holding of a good repute? For this purpose he often set before them and quoted the authority of the holy Scripture, and strongly encouraged them to copy sentences from the writings of the Saints. Furthermore, he gave them regular instruction in singing, taught them to attend the church assiduously, to honour Priests, to love religion, to hold converse with devout and learned men, to pray yet more often, and gladly to take their part in singing the praises of God. He himself was there present with cheerful countenance, directing the whole choir in their harmonious melody; and likewise on feast days he often played on the organ, rejoicing greatly in this task, and being herein a true imitator of David, that holy king who played upon the harp and danced before the ark of God, singing His praises. In process of time the fame of John Cele's goodness went forth to the utmost parts of Germany, and his sayings and opinions reached to the ends of the earth, borne thither on the lips of his pupils. The men of Brabant with the Flemings, they of Holland with the Frisians, they of Westphalia with the Saxons came in crowds to study under him, and having borne themselves studiously in the school, returned with their learning to their native places, men of Treves and Cologne, Liege and Utrecht, Kleef and Geldria were found here; and youths that were apt for learning gathered together from other villages and castles and made great progress in knowledge. The richer paid their own expenses out of their sufficiency, the poor gathered in bands to beg, giving thanks to the hands that helped them. These did the Master instruct gladly and without price when besought so to do for God's sake, for he was a true father of the needy, and he exhorted them to strive to turn their studies to God's service; but wandering and froward fellows he would not admit nor endure, but either by correction changed them to a better mind or drove them forth from his presence, lest the naughtiness of such presumptuous persons might work ill to them that were well disposed to obey, and disturb the peace of the studious flock and their Rector. So he was a rod of fear to the idle, but a staff of protection and safety to them that were well disposed to learn. Many of his hearers, when they had laid fitting foundation of knowledge, flew higher to loftier studies, and those who bore them diligently were promoted to the degree of Masters in a short while, and certain of these applying themselves to yet fuller knowledge were found worthy to be counted in the number of the Doctors.

The great city of Paris doth know, holy Cologne and Erfurt do confess, and the Curia at Rome is not ignorant of this, namely, the number of learned men whom the school of Zwolle sent forth while Master John Cele ruled her with all diligence, which thing he continued for a great while, even until his hair grew white, for they say that this venerable Master governed the scholars here for more than forty years.

This is his great glory, that so vast a multitude of his scholars speak well of him, so many illustrious Clerks praise him, so devout a company of monks still remember his name.

All things were well at Zwolle beneath his rule; they of the world were not at enmity with the scholars, the devout might serve God freely where they would, the Religious were under good supervision, and Priests of honest life were accepted of the citizens.

They who governed the people feared God and were endowed with wisdom and riches; moreover, amongst them were many learned magistrates who had been of old disciples of John, and as was fitting, they ever held him in love and reverence. He had collected many books for his own use, both of philosophy and divinity, and he directed that after his death these should be distributed for pious uses; for some he left as a pious bequest, and for the good of his own soul, to churches, some to monasteries, and some to the poor. So this is that revered and justly praised Master John Cele, a native of the town of Zwolle, a man well taught, learned, not puffed up by knowledge, sober, chaste, humble, and devout.

Once he had gone to the country of Brabant with the venerable Master Gerard Groote to see face to face that man most dear to God, John Ruesbroeck, one that was illustrious for his life and doctrine, for he had known him from afar, since his fame was noised abroad, and this journey he made out of love for his devout and holy life. John Ruesbroeck received them both in fatherly wise, and after a few days they returned to their own habitation, greatly refreshed by the words of his mouth and by his living example. This is more fully set forth in the book of the life of that memorable Father. From this time forth the flame of brotherly love burned yet more vehemently in the heart of each, and, indeed, John Cele did wondrously love Gerard from the very beginning of his preaching, ever holding him dear, and a man of one heart with him in Christ, one that did treat well of the Word of God before the people, showed a pattern of life in his own conduct, and was very fervent in his zeal for souls. For this reason Master John bore the reproach of men and much evil speaking from the froward, who never fail so to entreat them that do well; and this befell him because he encouraged and praised the acts of the Master and the glorious words of his preaching, yet was he not overcome by the snarls of envious folk, nor ceased greatly to extol Gerard, but before the magistrates and the people he spake freely on behalf of the Religious. To him did Gerard address certain friendly letters, and John, who loved the Master's words with all his heart, did collect the whole number of his epistles, because of his delight in reading them. Likewise he did often mention the venerable Master by name to his scholars, as one whom he knew well, and in his own pleasant voice did recount his deeds for an example to them. This is the end of the life of John, that faithful servant of Christ Jesus, to whom may God grant to enjoy the glory of heaven with all the saints. His body was buried at Windesem, in the ancient cloister, near the door of the church.

CHAPTER XXI.

Concerning John Brinckerinck, a disciple of Master Gerard.

In the year of the Lord 1419, on the 26th of March, that is to say, on the day following the Annunciation of the Blessed Virgin Mary, John Brinckerinck died at Deventer. He was a man beloved of God, a devout Priest and Rector, and Confessor to the Béguines in the House of Master Gerard Groote. He was born of good parents in the city of Zutphen, in Geldria, and in the years of his youth he began the devout life through the preaching of Master Gerard, for in a short while he became a disciple of the Master and was adorned with special grace; moreover, he heard many good things from him, and received from his mouth words of heavenly wisdom, for he oft held converse with him in the House, and yet more often without when they journeyed.

After Gerard's happy death, John was ordained to the priesthood, and when John de Gronde, the first Confessor of the Sisters at Deventer died, he ruled the said Sisterhood which Gerard had founded, being set up as the second Rector thereof, in which office he was a zealous minister, and he governed the Sisters in most excellent wise for many years, for God helped him. Sometimes he preached the Word of God in church to the people, and he drew many to the service of God as handmaids of Christ; and when the congregation of Sisters had begun to grow in merit and to increase daily in number, he began to build a monastery for the Nuns of the Order of Regulars outside the city of Deventer towards the north, a work done with great and daily labour, and he ruled the same most strictly with all diligence.

Through his example and his counsels, which promoted the salvation of many, a great number of other Houses for Nuns were begun in divers parts, of which some were under the discipline of the Canons Regular, while others professed the rule of the third Order and were incorporated therein.

His body was taken to his own monastery at Diepenvene, and there buried in the choir before the High Altar, and after his death John Hoef was preferred to be Rector of the Sisters in Deventer, but the care of the Nuns was committed to the Prior of Windesem.

CHAPTER XXII.

Of the death of Gisbert Dou, Rector of the Sisters at Amsterdam.

In the year of the Lord 1420, on the day before the Feast of the Nativity of the glorious Virgin Mary, Gisbert Dou died in Holland. He was a Priest of reverend life and Rector and Confessor to many Sisters in Amsterdam, and he did also promote and found two monasteries for the Canons Regular. This man of God, from the beginning of his conversion, was very familiar with Gerard Groote, and his close friend, for he knew his inmost thoughts better than did any other mortal man, both the good thoughts and the bad alike, and whatever Gerard did in his life, for he was his Confessor and his most faithful confidant in those things which pertain to the examination of the conscience. He held with him, therefore, most devout colloquies, frequently conferring with him as to the condition of the Brothers or Sisters, and the things needful to preserve the devotion which had begun in many places. But through the bounty of God he lived safely for many years to comfort the good, and he often preached the Word of God publicly in the church to the people. He was kindly and liberal in hospitality to all who came to him, a faithful helper of the poor, a sweet comforter to the sad, a staunch friend to the Religious. The mighty looked favourably upon him, the simple folk and the community loved him, and learned men and prelates heard him reverently; and so having fulfilled seventy-five years of life, he died in a good old age amongst the Fathers of his House, and was buried in the Convent of the Sisters of our Order.

In the year of the Lord 1450, Peter de Mera, Chamberlain to our Lord Eugenius IV, obtained a letter granting Indulgence to our House, namely, to the Prior, the Brothers, the Converts, the Donates, and the Oblates in the House on Mount St. Agnes; and the purport of his letter was as followeth:

"Most blessed Father and most holy Lord, This petition is made to further the salvation of the souls of your devout servants

Theodoric the Prior, the Canons or Brothers, and the other members of the community who dwell in the Monastery on Mount St. Agnes, near Zwolle, following the rule of the Order of Canons Regular, which monastery is in the diocese of Utrecht: likewise on behalf of the servants of this same House, and of other Priors, Canons, Brothers, members of the community, and servants, who shall dwell from time to time in the aforesaid monastery; wherefore that in future they may be ordered in more wholesome wise we beseech your holiness to deign of your grace to grant them Indulgence to the effect following, namely, that as long as they continue in the verity of the faith, the unity of the Holy Roman Church, in obedience and in devotion to your holiness and your successors, the Chief Pontiffs of the Holy Roman Church, who shall be canonically elected, so long a suitable Confessor chosen by them shall have power under the authority of the Apostolic See to grant to them when in articulo mortis full remission of all sin which they may have confessed with contrition of heart. Provided always that they presume not to do any unlawful thing through their reliance upon this Indulgence, and provided also that so soon as they are notified of this Indulgence they keep fast on every Friday for one whole year, or do some other act of piety: but if they have neglected to fast or been unable to do so, or if it hath been their custom heretofore so to fast on every Friday, then they shall be bound to perform some other special act of grace in accordance with the directions of the aforesaid Confessor.

"The privilege desired in this petition is granted to all professed Brothers, Converts, and Oblates, under perpetual vows, so long as they live in the observance of the rule.

"Given in the presence of our Lord the Pope,
"C. ARMINIENSIS.

"It is asked also that the aforesaid licence hold good without letters Apostolic to confirm the same.
"Granted. C. ARMINIENSIS."

CHAPTER XXIII.

As to the gaining of Indulgences at the stations in Rome.

To the venerable and devout Priors at Windesem and Mount St. Agnes near Zwolle, and to the Priests and Fathers unfeignedly beloved in Christ Jesus, these, from Brother Everard Swane of the House of the Blessed Virgin in the Wood near Northorn, your unprofitable servant, good Fathers. Venerable Fathers, most beloved in Christ Jesus, my love is ever ready to serve you, and I was desired by divers persons, yea, and besought, as I understood, by some of your Brothers also, to write to the Curia to enquire as to the virtue and extent of the Indulgences granted at certain stations in Rome by our most Holy Father Pope Eugenius IV, the granting of which Indulgences was promoted by my Lord the Cardinal as ye do know. I was required to ask the virtue of such, and how they might be obtained; this thing, therefore, I did long since, and I have received a reply to this effect, namely: "That no man may know fully the virtue and extent of these Indulgences, because from the time of St. Peter onward, Indulgences beyond number have been given and granted by divers Pontiffs."

I have spoken likewise on this matter with certain persons that are about the Court, and to put the matter shortly, these also are unable to give any certain decision in the matter, but, arguing it amongst themselves, some said that the remission of all sins may be obtained at any station; others held and said that all Indulgences granted throughout the whole city may be obtained at any one of the stations. Which is the truer argument I dare not to say, beloved Fathers, but this I know full well of mine own knowledge and experience, that Cardinals, Prelates, and others, both men and women, throughout the whole city, are wont to be zealous in visiting each several station; neither is it the usage there to make any reference to the virtue or extent of the Indulgences, even inwardly, but every man doth commit this matter to God Who alone doth know the tale of the same, and we too ought to follow this custom. But as concerning the gaining of the same, of which I have made mention above, the Chamberlain of my Lord Bologna, who returned to this country a short while ago for divers purposes, hath told me thereof by word of mouth, and he saith that he himself was present when the Indulgences were granted. Every man that hath made his confession and is contrite, and hath fulfilled the conditions laid down in the letter wherein the Indulgence was granted—that is, living in common and in the observance of the rule—may gain the same in the church of his own monastery. And these conditions are that he enter the church with the same intention that he would have in Rome were he present there on the proper days for visiting the stations; that he prostrate himself before the altar which he would have chosen there, and pour forth his prayers or certain repetitions of the Pater Noster as devoutly as he may: that he celebrate Mass: or visit the several altars saying the Pater Noster or other prayers after the same manner as that which is customary in the aforesaid city. In short, if any man doth as is aforesaid, there is sure hope that he will gain the Indulgences just as if he were actually present in Rome, as is set forth also in the said letter. Therefore, beloved Fathers, ye may, if it please you, tell these things to the Brothers of your House, or to any others ye will that desire to be informed as to the matters set forth above, and in this do as may seem expedient to you. As for our Lord Eugenius the Pope, aforementioned, who hath granted and given us Indulgences so freely, and my Lord of Bologna who procured the grant, and others who have laboured in what manner soever to this same end, ye will (as they do trust) make mention of them in your prayers, especially on the days proper for the stations, committing them to God for the sake of Jesus the humble. And may He see fit to keep you, and all that are committed to your charge, safe in His holy service.

Written on the day following the Feast of St. Philip and St. James, in the year of the Lord 1443.

CHAPTER XXIV.

The letter of the Cardinal of Bologna.

Antony, by the mercy of God, Bishop of Ostia, Cardinal of the Holy Roman Church, and commonly known as the Cardinal of Bologna, to all and each of the Canons Regular, our beloved in Christ, and to all other persons that are Converts or Lay Brothers in the House of the Blessed Virgin in the Wood, and in the Houses elsewhere that belong to the said Order of St. Augustine in whatever diocese they may be, and who live in the observance of the rule, and to others who shall see these presents, greeting:

It is a just thing, and one consonant with reason, to bear witness to the truth; wherefore by the tenor of these presents we do notify your whole society, and bear witness that our most holy Father and Lord Eugenius IV, by divine providence Pope, by his Apostolic authority hath granted to each and all of you Indulgence and Concession following at my prayer and instance, the same being delivered by word of mouth and needing no further confirmation by letters Apostolic. Ye are not bound in any way whatever to avoid any man, even though he be for the time being held under sentence of excommunication, either at the time of the celebration of the divine Mysteries or at other seasons (unless indeed there be any in your churches that are publicly denounced as excommunicate), nor shall such intercourse be held to impute guilt to you or to any one of your company. Likewise and by similar authority he doth grant to you, that those among you that for the time being do suffer infirmities in the body be not bound to say or recite the Canonical Hours during the time of such infirmity, nor be deemed to be under such compulsion so that they be excused by the counsel of such suitable Confessors as may be chosen from your body.

Likewise that each Prelate of your several churches shall have authority with regard to vows to make pilgrimage across the seas, to the shrine of the Blessed Peter and Paul, or other places of pilgrimage which ought to be paid by you, or any one of you, from time to time, to commute the same to other acts of piety.

Furthermore and by the authority aforesaid he doth grant to the followers of your devotion this concession:

Whereas Indulgences have been granted by the Apostolic See to faithful persons all and sundry who from year to year devoutly visit certain churches in the which "stations" are appointed for certain days—and of these churches some are within, and some without the city—and whereas these Indulgences are granted to persons who visit the said churches on the days for which stations for this purpose are appointed;

Now therefore he doth grant that each and all of you, being truly penitent and having made confession, may and ought to enjoy the benefits of such Indulgences just as if ye had actually and in person visited the churches aforesaid.

And this concession shall avail both for the present and time to come for ever, so that it hold good for those of you only who shall continue to live in common, and in your own community (that is under the General Chapter), and shall persevere in the observance of the said rule.

A LETTER CONCERNING THE FIRST INSTITUTION OF THE MONASTERY AT WINDESEM.

Here beginneth the preface to the work following: with the whole affection of my heart and mind, and with the service of my voice do I exalt God, the Invisible, the Almighty, and His only begotten son our Lord Jesus Christ.

My most beloved Brother of old, when I told the tale of the former state of this House, of the Fathers and Brothers thereof, and their blessed deeds, and when I related also the origin of this foundation, thou didst seem to lend an ear somewhat readily thereto. Furthermore, thou didst make request that some memorial thereof should be committed to writing (for so it seemed good to thee), because they who saw and knew the former members of the House and the fervour of their lives, are now almost all dead; and I am as it were the dregs of the cup, the very last of all; and being already worn with age, it is like that I shall not be suffered to abide long with thee. For this cause thou dost affirm that it should be profitless and wasteful that by the lapse of time things that might perchance serve as an example and tend to the edification of some, should pass over to forgetfulness.

Wherefore I have fulfilled thy petition, though mayhap not thy full desire, since my manner of writing is coarse and ill-kempt; for which reason I have made no mention of thy name, nor of my own; and this is of set purpose lest if this poor letter fall at any time into the hands of another, he might be offended on the very threshold and so not care to go forward any further.

II.

The history of the origin of the New Devotion.

Now in the days of old the land of the English did abound in men great and holy, by whose saintliness and doctrine (as saith the venerable Bede) that land was watered like the Paradise of the Lord; and so it was that certain rivulets of that water, through the mercy of God, flowed down to this our land to make it fruitful. For this country was up to that time truly parched and ill-tended, inasmuch as doing service to idols, and being ensnared in the errors of the heathen, it was held captive of the devil.

III.

Of them by whom this land was turned to the Faith of Christ.

As for the first and chief of these spiritual rivulets, namely that great man and true saint, Willebrord, we know the tale of how he appeared here by sure testimony. For in the time of Pepin, King of the Franks, and his son Charles the Great, and when 700 years more or less had elapsed since the birth of the Lord, Willebrord with eleven others did irrigate the said land with the waters of their holy preaching. Moreover, with the help of his companions he did busy himself with breaking up the ground with the ploughshare of discipline, yet not without much difficulty; and in a short space the task of spreading the faith did prosper wondrously beneath their hands; for God worked with them, and did confirm their words with signs following.

Of a truth how great a fervour of faith and devotion flourished in this our land under their guidance, and for a long while after their days, is shown to this day, not only by the testimony of the books which we have read, but also by those countless churches and monasteries which, as we see, were builded on every side where the temples of idols had been overthrown.

IV.

A lamentation over the waning of the aforesaid fervour.

But, fie upon it, this first fervour and regular observance of discipline did in process of time grow so lukewarm and feeble, that the outward framework thereof alone remained, and as for the fruitfulness of the truly spiritual life, the devil might seem to have said in the words of Esaias, "and with the sole of my feet have I dried up all the rivers of defence."

A certain aged man and an honoured priest spake in my hearing of this drouth and failure of devotion, and referring to the time of which I tell, he said that in the days of his youth and in these parts of the Low Countries, all things pertaining to devotion and charity were so brought to nothingness, that if any were touched inwardly by a desire to amend his life, he would scarce find one single man from whom to ask counsel; nor scarce one spot where he could put these fledgling desires into a place of safety, unless it were among the Carthusians; for amongst them Religious observance and the vigour of spiritual life did flourish at that time, but scarce amongst any others.

V.

Of the rise of the New Devotion in our land.

Since, therefore, there was such drouth throughout the whole land (as hath been said before) that there seemed to be no trace anywhere of the ancient devotion, the good Lord looked down from Heaven upon the earth with the eye of His mercy, and made rise a little fount in these failing days and in our land that was desert, pathless, and unwatered; which fount grew by little and little to be a river (as is said in the Book of Esther), and after a while into much water to irrigate not trees that are corruptible, but souls, which truly are the plants of that garden which is of the Spirit and faileth not.

VI.

Of Master Gherard Groet.

Master Gherard Groet was this memorable fount, and not unworthily is he thus typified, having been small in his lowly esteem and abnegation of himself, but as his name doth signify, in the sight of God mighty to overthrow by the sword of this word of the Lord the foes that rise up against the salvation of His elect, so that he and his beloved sons might gain the inheritance of Israel. One may say fitly enough of this man what St. Augustine saith of Paulinus, who from being very rich became for God's sake very poor and yet with full store of holiness.

Moreover, like Anah, he found the hot springs in the desert, namely, the sweetness of divine love beyond common measure, together with abundant zeal to gain souls, and an hatred of wickedness.

Having these things before his eyes he spared not while he lived either toil or cost, for he went about preaching everywhere in hunger and thirst, in cold and nakedness.

VII.

Of his death.

At length after much strife, and having converted many to Christ, this most blessed Father passed happily to the Lord in the year of the Lord 1384; and he left the residue of the work, of which he himself had done enough, to his little ones, those whom he had gathered under his wings that they might promote the salvation of many and be their pattern, whom also he had nurtured with the milk of his goodness and his sweet-savoured doctrine; for it was his intention that through them should be finished that work which he had ever in mind, and had striven to carry into effect so far as he could; namely, to snatch souls from the jaws of the devil and restore them to their Maker. This work his followers in their time were not backward to do, neither have their successors to the present day ceased to fulfil the same task.

VIII.

Concerning Florentius and his companions.

Of these primitive disciples of Master Gherard, the first and chief was that Florentius, son of Radewin, who was wonderful in all holiness and honesty of character, and whose name that House, which was the first of all the congregations of Clerks only, doth still retain. In like manner one House at Deventer still hath its name from Gherard Groet, because it was the House wherein he dwelt, and afterward this was the first of all the congregations of women. This Florentius with his companions that were men of light, and whose names and deeds are of record, made no small gain of souls for the Lord, especially amongst the scholars that were Clerks, and by their labours the monasteries of divers orders were propped up in no slight degree and reformed also, the Lord working by their means.

IX.

How like things were done in other cities.

Florentius seeing that this was good, and that indeed no sacrifice could be more acceptable to God than zeal for souls, sent devout and learned men to other cities also to do a like work, especially to places where there were schools largely attended, such as Zwolle, Doesborch, Herderwijc and the like; and these men lived a common life like that in the congregation already founded, and gained their livelihood by writing books. They studied most of all to draw to Christ such scholars as were Clerks and when they were so drawn and converted, to send them to the several monasteries and congregations, there to serve the Lord. Moreover, the conversion of these and their conversation was a cause and means of salvation to many, as we found out afterward in the case of divers of them. So much of their calling Clerks to Christ.

X.

Of the names of the Fathers and Rectors of the first congregation.

Furthermore, with regard to the Fathers of the former congregations (to go back a little to my former subject), I, in the hearing of Christ Jesus, without whom nothing can be begun or founded duly, do say as followeth:

"Through what act of grace or miracle came it to pass that as Master Gherard Groet was preaching and sowing the seed everywhere, there were added to him so suddenly and unexpectedly men of such kind and so great, for these were of one mind with him, and every one of them in each city and place burned with the zeal with which he also burned to exhort and convert a people that was stiff necked. Yet with all diligence they set them to the task of gathering together virgins as pearls from the shells and most pure lilies from the thorns. These were in their days true bridesmen and friends of the bridegroom, who hear and rejoice because of the bridegroom's voice: who strove with emulation in God's behalf to present the whole body of plighted virgins whom they had gathered together as one chaste virgin to one husband, even to Christ.

Thou dost ask, perhaps, "Who are they whom thou dost so commend, and what are their names?" Hear then:

In Deventer, John Brinckerinc ruled over the virgins that were first gathered together there, and from these in after days sprang the House at Dyepenween, which was under the same Rector.

In Zutphen was Henry of Huesden; in Doesborch, Tric Gruter; in Zwolle, Henry of Gouda; in Kampen, Tric of Gramsberch; in Utrecht, Werembold. In Amersfoort, William son of Henry; in Leyden, Peter of Poel; in Harlem, Hugo Goltsmit; in Amsterdam, Ghijsbert of Oude; in Horn, Paul of Medenblic. Likewise in Enchusen, Paul of that city; in Pormereynde, Nicolas of that city; in Almelo, Everard of Eza;

likewise in Schutdorp, Henry of that city. These are the holy men whom the Lord chose with love unfeigned to carry on and complete His work which Master Gherard Groet had begun in wholesome wise by His inspiration, as hath been set forth already. Holiness made them priests, learning made them doctors, diligence made them profitable rectors of many congregations, and zeal for the gaining of souls made them notable preachers as hath been found in the case of many of them. O happy day on which that great Gherard was born amongst us, for he was the fount and source whence flowed the waters of salvation to our land, so that what before his time had been parched became a pool, and the thirsty land, springs of water.

XI.

Of the multiplication of the devout, especially of virgins.

From this time forth the fount that once was small began to grow by means of the rivulets aforesaid into abundant waters, that is, monasteries without number and congregations also which fed them, so that it should seem that the saying in Exodus was fulfilled which saith of the sons of Israel how that when Joseph died his seed was multiplied exceedingly and filled the land. Thus it came to pass that the people, both men and women, loved a life of virginity, and in chastity emulated the dwellers in Heaven. But above all there was a vast band of women that were virgins who despised the thought of motherhood, and spurned this flowery world with contempt, ever showing by their thoughts, their deeds, and their bearing, that they desired rather to be united to that Spouse Who is in Heaven. What state is there to-day, what township or city in the whole province of Cologne but rejoiceth to have known the savour and scent of these same lilies? Yet was there diversity in their lots, for as Paul doth testify of himself, so too was it with them; some having a savour of life unto life, and some a savour of death unto death. But in this the matter of their election is most clearly shown, and likewise the fact that they were not of the world, because they ever bare the world's hatred and persecution, sometimes suffering at the hands of parents and kindred, sometimes from rulers and the common folk of the cities and towns, beneath which persecution they bore themselves with all patience and humility; yet they suffered most greatly from false teachers and preachers who were zealous to assail with mad words, and to persecute a manner of life that they knew not, yet did not they not prevail.

XII.

How a certain monk of Cologne was put to confusion.

For example, one such was preaching in Cologne at the time of the Prague heresy, and he said among other matter: "Ye do go to Prague to contend with heretics whom ye might find readily in your midst—even in St. Gereon's Street"—by which he signified the Sisters of the congregation who dwelt in the said street. But the great ones of the city took the word very ill, saying that such a thing was never heard, namely, that heretics should dwell in the fair city of Cologne. But why should I say more? At length the matter was referred to the bishops and to the university, and, save that the monk had somewhat speedily sought refuge by flight, it would have conduced to his own detriment that he ever preached that word in Cologne.

XIII.

How the Sisters were examined.

Forthwith Master Henry de Gorinchem was sent to enquire into the charge of the false preacher aforesaid (for this Master Henry was held in the highest esteem among theologians at that time), and he did skilfully perform the task assigned to him, examining the affairs and condition of those Sisters with all diligence, and when he understood clearly their sincerity in the Faith; their obedience in all things to Holy Church; how that they had given up all personal property both in goods and in their own will; their chastity and how in all things they did imitate the Mother of Christ; their patience in watching, fasting, and in seeking to gain their whole sustenance by the labour of their hands, he was astonished thereat and returning to those who had sent him he spake openly, saying, "If this life be not that in which every Christian ought to follow Christ, then have I never read the Scriptures." And from that time he bore such goodwill toward them, that very often he would help them in their suits, and likewise by his will he distributed notable gifts amongst them.

XIV.

Concerning Master Bernard de Reyda.

Next in order there was the disciple and successor of this doctor, namely, Master Bernard de Reyda, who may fittingly be reckoned amongst the most illustrious, and he ruled over the Sisters aforesaid until the present day, being also their Confessor and Fellow Commoner. But whither have we come? Verily it was our purpose, according to thy petition to say somewhat of the first members of our House at Windesem for thy delectation: but I do confess I have been led further than I thought by my desire to bring forth into the light the names of the Fathers aforementioned who were well known to me, fearing lest in process of time they should be hidden altogether in the darkness of silence, which thing God forbid. But in the second place, the savour of these sweet-scented lilies that were now spread far and wide amid the monasteries and congregations, did compel me to bear some testimony as to their number and their most holy conversation, while the breath of life is yet whole in me. For unworthy though I be, I have conversed with them for these many years past, visiting and holding colloquies with them, and I have ever found them firm in the faith, and in deed effectual; wherefore let any man say what he will of them, but I say with Balaam: "Let me die the death of the Righteous, and let my last end be like theirs"—but let us return to the purpose whence we have wandered.

XV.

Of the origin of the House at Windesem.

So under Florentius and his companions there grew a great company of devout persons, both Clerks and Laics, who either wished to dwell with them or at least relied upon their wholesome admonition and counsel.

Amongst these were two men of no mean rank according to worldly dignity, sagacious in mind and sufficiently learned for their degree, namely Henry de Wilsen, a citizen of Kampen, and Goswin Tyasen, a citizen of Zwolle. These two, being prudent men and well skilled in worldly matters, were a strong stay to Florentius and his companions, and ever present helpers in all the work that the Lord had ordained should be done through them.

But when they saw how, that after the death of Master Gherard Groet of holy memory, the heavens continually dropped honey, and how that from the seed which Gherard had planted and the skies bedewed from above, many congregations of men and women began to spring up on every side, they rejoiced with exceeding joy; also they began to hold many colloquies amongst themselves, as to how this good beginning that had its wholesome origin from God might continue unshaken for a yet longer space to His glory, and the salvation of many souls.

They found by God's inspiration that this might be done by the means following, that is to say, if a monastery of some approved order, but preferably of the Canons Regular, should be founded, under whose shadow all the devout turtle-doves might have a secure refuge from the swoop of the falcon. But where might a place be found, and the other things also that were needful for the carrying out of such a work? For, as saith the Apostle of the calling of the primitive Church, so amongst these also there were not many rich, not many noble—save them that their virtue did make noble and them that voluntary poverty did make rich before God.

Wherefore these Converts prayed to the Lord with all their hearts, that He, without whom no good thing is begun, carried forward, or ended, might deign effectually to show them what might be His good pleasure in this business; and they remembered likewise that Master Gherard Groet ever kept the same purpose in mind, although he could not carry his desire into effect, for death was beforehand with him.

XVI.

Concerning Brother Bertold, and the site of this monastery.

The Lord therefore, that He might show how He was the cause and the beginner of all these things, stirred up the spirit of a young Clerk named Bertold ten Hove, who was the owner of broad meadows, and particularly of an estate that is called "Hof to Windesem"—where by God's aid we now do dwell—and he, coming to Florentius and his company, did of his own act and free will offer to give himself and all his possessions into their hands for the service of God, and he desired earnestly that a monastery might be builded in the aforesaid place, if this might be done.

When they knew this, all betook them to praising God, reaching up their hands toward Heaven; for they held it as a most sure sign that He had heard their prayer, and had promised to be, by some means or other, the promoter of this cause. Straightway so many of them as were owners of houses or lands sold them and put the price into Florentius' hands, or at least resigned the same for the use of the monastery that should be builded.

XVII.

Of the goodwill and consent of Florentius the Lord Bishop.

Forthwith they began to be instant with the venerable Lord Florentius of Wevelichoven, who was then Bishop of Utrecht, for his consent to the founding of a monastery, and for the privileges needful for this business; and him they found most gracious in all things, for he had a special love of virtue.

This was done in the year of the Lord 1386, and by the co-operation of God (good men also reaching forth an hand to help them) the affair so prospered that in the year following, that is in 1387, on the day following the Feast of St. Gallus the Confessor, an humble church and burial-ground and also four altars were consecrated in due order by Hubert, the venerable Bishop of Yppuse, in honour of the Holy Trinity, and the Blessed Virgin and others.

XVIII.

Of the first Brothers of this monastery.

But since it is written, "Not the people for the place's sake, but the place for the people's sake," we must see who were the first to dwell here; since indeed these were the founders and the pattern of all who did afterwards come under the Chapter of Windesem.

In the first place there was Henry of Uxaria, at that time the only priest amongst them, and he was appointed Rector by the Bishop, by whose commission the said Henry received the Religious habit from the suffragan.

Next there was Henry de Wilsen and Goswin Tyasen, who were invested as Clerks, that did devote themselves, for they would not be promoted to holy orders by reason of a stain that did unfit them under the rule. Also there were these following: Brother John of Huesden, Brother Henry Wilde, Brother Werner Keencamp, Brother Bertold ten Hove, Brother John Kempis, and Brother Henry Balveren. All these were sons and disciples of Florentius, from whose breast they sucked in abundance the milk of all goodness, which same they poured forth without stint for their posterity in after days.

These men and certain others of the community, whose will was good thereto, were marked out by Florentius to build the monastery in the place aforesaid, and to take the habit of Holy Religion therein to the Glory of Christ; which task they were forward to fulfil with wisdom and all speed; also to the men above named there were added, a short space afterward, certain persons of like intention and fervour, namely, John Otto of Zoes, Henry Loder, Arnold of Kalkar, Gherard of Naeldwijc, John of Broechusen, and others.

XIX.

The praise of the early Fathers.

O Windesem, these are they by whom thy first foundations were laid, through whom was kindled that bright light, namely, the rule of the truly Regular life; so that thou who wast then as a grain of mustard seed, the least of all herbs, wast enabled to grow into a great tree, beneath the shadow of whose branches fowls of heaven, without number, might take their pleasant rest.

XX.

How the Brothers aforesaid were promoted in other monasteries.

At last when many houses that sprung from the same stock had been founded on all sides, both for men and women, there was scarce one of them but desired that a pastor might be provided from amongst the aforesaid Brothers of Windesem.

This we did see with our own eyes and hear in after days, how Brother Henry of Uxaria was appointed by the Bishops to be the first Rector of this House, which office he held for but a short time; then we did see Brother John of Huesden, a young man in years but hoary in mind, who ruled this church of ours for above thirty-three years in wholesome wise, to the great increase of our goods, both spiritual and temporal, and was beloved of God and man. When he died Brother Gherard Naeldwijc was chosen by all the Brothers to take the place of the departed Prior, yet scarce for half a year could he bear the honour and burden of this care by reason of his exceeding lowliness, but he renounced the office of Prior and cast off the burden thereof in presence of all the Brothers, though this was contrary to the opinion of the whole community, and likewise to that of the Fathers gathered together in the Chapter.

Likewise we have seen how Henry Wilde was chosen to be Prior at Eemsteyn, Brother Werner at Horn, Brother John Kempis at Mount St. Agnes, Brother Arnold Kalkar at the Fount of the Blessed Mary, Brother John Otto at Amsterdam, Brother Henry Loder at Northorn, Brother John Broechusen at Leerdorp, and so forth.

XXI.

Of the pattern of virtue left for us by the Fathers.

And now, in the last place, one must see how virtuous were these men, and what an example they left for us to imitate. But no one amongst men knoweth the things of a man, save the spirit of a man which is in him; yet by considering his outward deeds one may guess what lieth hidden inwardly in him.

XXII.

Of their simplicity and poverty.

One may know by the humble plan of the former House which they builded how greatly these men loved simplicity and holy poverty. For the inner walls thereof were small, and the House was covered in with reeds or thatch; so at that time what is now the part behind the church was the whole church itself; and the chapel that is now was then the refectory; the brewery was the kitchen, and the old brewery was our mill house and infirmary. Moreover, the bounds of the monastery were so narrow that the present inner wall on the north of the barn was then the extreme outer wall of the House. So the whole was lowly and small, being arranged to receive but few inmates.

XXIII.

Of their Victual.

They kept a frugal and poor table, not so much of necessity, or through lack, as out of love of poverty, and the habit which was implanted in them, which same they had acquired together with the disciples of Florentius.

So on a time I heard Brother Gherard Naeldwijc say in pleasantry that in those times on fast days they would sometimes divide one fig into four or six portions that so the great quantity of the bread they consumed might be seasoned by those fragments. On a time also there come to us, I know not whence, half a jar of salted salmon, and as the Brothers were doubting what should be done therewith, Brother Henry de Wilsen, being ever greatly zealous for discipline, persuaded them that by all means it ought to be sold lest such new and unaccustomed dainties should begin to be brought in.

At this time they had no flocks of sheep, nor any fishery, nor fishers, but so piously and soberly did they live that Gherard of Bronchorst, a Canon of St. Saviour's, who once sojourned for a while with the Brothers at Windesem, was wont to say in his own pleasant manner, "None fare sumptuously in Windesem unless it be the swine and the guests." So also to drink wine and eat roast fowls were held in Windesem to be matters that should be referred to the Bishop.

XXIV.

Of their Vesture.

Their vesture and their utensils were notable examples of their true lowliness and simplicity, so that I remember to have seen those venerable elders, Brother Henry of Uxaria and Brother Henry de Wilsen, wearing garments that were altogether worn through by constantly rubbing against the seats as they leaned back, and these were botched about the elbows with great patches of rough cloth. But if men of their quality wore such vesture what wonder if the younger men in those days were not more freakish than they in the matter of clothing?

Indeed, I lie if I have not seen some of our household that were Laics wearing sad-coloured garments made of bark fibre, in providing which and like garments also Brother Henry Balveren, the Vestiarius, showed great zeal, as did the tailor, Brother Herbert, a Convert who was formerly a disciple of Gherard Groet.

They had likewise certain hair shirts which were lent from time to time to divers of the younger Brothers for the taming of their vices and concupiscence, and one of these was as rough as those hair cloths with which the brewers' cauldrons are wont to be dried.

XXV.

How they avoided all occasion of scandal.

One may see how greatly they preferred their own good report and the edification of all men before all worldly good, by this tale; namely, that on a time two young men of Deventer came to Windesem, of whom one was called Goswin Comhaer (a man who was afterward a great example), but the other was Conrad Mom. These earnestly sought to be received here, but the members of the House made answer saying that in this region there would be too much talk if this were done, and if they remained in this place, for their parents dwelt hard by: let them rather go to Eemsteyn. And receiving this reply the men took it ill enough, so that I heard one of them exclaim in a sad voice: "May God pity us in that we cannot obtain or know any place of rest for this cause, namely, that we are rich." And they went obediently to Eemsteyn.

XXVI.

Of their Charity.

These men also were wondrous charitably disposed toward all that did lack, especially toward new Houses of our own order that were begun in poverty. These they desired to help to an extent even beyond their power, by transferring to them both goods and men, as is manifest not only in the matter of the two youths aforementioned, but also in the case of divers others that were rich and desired to dwell with them. These they did often direct to other monasteries to relieve their needs, for they sought not what might be profitable to themselves, but rather what should be so to others. Thus they sent Arnold Droem to Mount St. Agnes, Stephen Wael to the Valley of Peace, and Brother Nicholas Bochorst to Nazareth, and so forth.

In like manner it was agreed by the community with regard to Brother John ten Water that he should be sent to the Fount of the Blessed Mary where there seemed to be notable scarcity; yet by his lowliness and his great importunity that he should by no means be parted from the Brothers, he did overcome this resolution.

But the well spring of their goodness ceased not with these, rather it did flow forth and reach all men, especially poor Clerks and members of the Houses of the New Devotion. What man did ever return from them empty-handed? for if the petitioner were rich, he brought back counsel, if he were poor he received help.

XXVII.

Concerning Gherard of Renen.

There was in those days, that is, amongst the first Fathers, a man of great age, who was by no means the least of his own folk, and his name was Gherard of Renen. He would sojourn for long spaces of time with the Brothers at Windesem, for he was bound to them by an exceeding love: and being on a time in the House at Utrecht wherein I dwelt, and in the presence of a certain honourable matron who was his kinswoman, he began to speak of the aforesaid Brothers, their manner of life and their virtues, and I myself was there present also. So then this woman was suddenly kindled to so great fervour by the things that she had heard that she suddenly burst forth with these words: "Ah, if I were a man, and mine own master, no one should hinder me from going to such a community." And I verily believe that until this man told his tale I myself had never heard mention of Windesem.

XXVIII.

Of the privileges obtained for the binding together of the Chapters.

After a short while it came to pass that three daughters were born to the House at Windesem, namely Eemsteyn, the House of the Blessed Virgin, and the House of the New Light near Horn. And when in this manner the number of the monasteries had grown to four, by the advice of Florentius and the other Fathers aforenamed, they sent to the Curia at Rome in the time of Boniface the Pope, who granted them leave to gather together a General Chapter together with authority and fitting privileges and so forth; for up to this time they had agreed to remain directly under the rule of the Bishop. Gherard of Bronchorst, who hath been named above, did take upon him this mission with all devotion, but Reyner Minnenbode, the founder of the monastery at Eemsteyn paid, as it is said, all the expenses thereof in most liberal wise.

XXIX.

Of their manner of holding the Chapter.

But when the Fathers and Brothers of these four Houses held a Chapter in their humble fashion, the Fathers of the congregations whose names are given above would come together, or at least some of them, and sit them down to deal with matters concerning not the acquiring of worldly wealth, but the conversion of souls and the maintenance of the common good. And at that time all were as it were one fold and one flock, and in very deed one body in Christ.

XXX.

The Conclusion.

What sayest thou to these things now, Brother most beloved, remembering that thou wast a wild olive, and meet for eternal fire, and seeing that thou art now grafted, in despite of nature, on this fair and fruitful olive tree, and art become a partaker in its fatness? Canst thou do aught save proclaim with the whole inward love of thine heart, "Great is thy mercy to me, O Lord, and Thou hast snatched my soul from the nethermost Hell"? For it is written of Catho that he would praise his gods mightily—he being but an heathen—and extol his own good fortune, in that it had been permitted to him to be born in that land, and at that time when he could see Rome and her Empire flourishing in the height of their prosperity; and if this is true, Brother most beloved, what return wilt thou make to the Lord thy God for that it was given thee to be born and to live in this time of His Most abundant Goodness, and in a land which He, the Lord, hath blessed? Hadst thou lived in the days of thy fathers, before our land was illumined by the light of Grace of which so much hath been said already, what else could have befallen but that thou shouldest have done even as they did? From which it doth follow that thou also wouldest have gone even whither they went, there to abide for ever.

O happy days in which were born the leaders and chiefs of this new army of ours, I mean Gherard Groet and Florentius, and their son's sons also, and they that are born from them continually! and so it shall continue to the end of time. Amen. May the Mother of Grace grant thee to follow their footsteps and to hold fast their doctrine.

※ ※ ※ ※ ※

Here endeth the letter concerning the first institutors of the monastery at Windesem, which letter was written by the venerable Father William Voern.

www.ingramcontent.com/pod-product-compliance
Lightning Source LLC
Chambersburg PA
CBHW071607170426
43196CB00034B/2180